FILL GRAMMAR GAPS

Shareen Mayers

Year 6

Teach tricky grammar topics in context

Ensure all pupils are fully prepared for the National Tests using creative ways to teach tricky and uninspiring grammar topics in context.

This book is divided into 15 topics focusing on word, sentence and text aspects from the KS1 and KS2 English National Curriculum and can be used for whole-class activities or for intervention/booster groups.

- **Detailed teaching notes** allow you to:
  - **'Review'** – catch-up, review and recap learning to fill gaps in grammar knowledge.
  - **'Teach'** – model example text extracts and sentences to spark classroom discussion.
  - **'Practise'** – use the interactive program to consolidate learning.
  - **'Apply'** – apply creative teaching ideas to make grammar lessons fun and engaging.

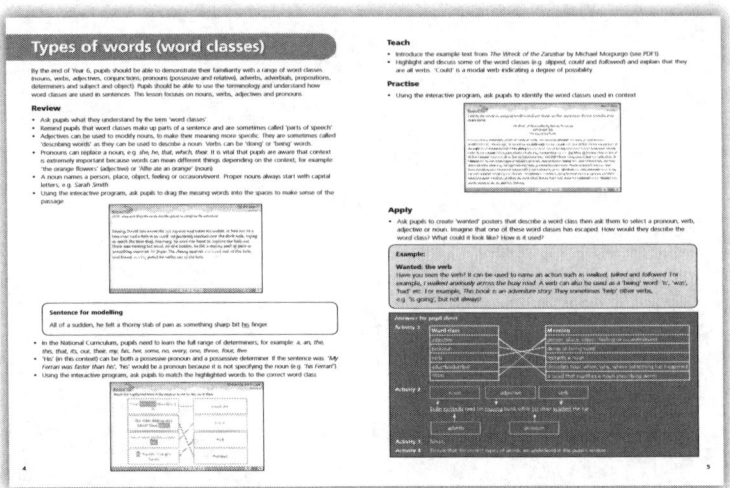

- **Pupil activity sheets** – for extra practice in the classroom or as consolidation for homework.
- **Text extracts** – 15 quality text extracts (PDFs) to display on a whiteboard to help teach grammar in context and save preparation time.
- **Interactive activities** – three accompanying interactive activities per topic to reinforce grammar concepts.
- **Answers** – answers to the pupil activities provided at the end of the teaching notes for easy reference.
- **Editable files** – teaching notes and pupil sheets on CD-ROM for maximum flexibility.

Published by Keen Kite Books
An imprint of HarperCollins*Publishers* Ltd
1 London Bridge Street
London SE1 9GF

ISBN 9780008203825

First published in 2016

10 9 8 7 6 5 4 3 2 1

Text & Design © 2016 Keen Kite Books, an imprint of HarperCollins*Publishers* Ltd

Images: © Shutterstock.com

All rights reserved. No part of this publication may be reproduced, stored in a retrieval system, or transmitted, in any form or by any means, electronic, mechanical, photocopying, recording or otherwise, without the prior permission of Keen Kite Books.

British Library Cataloguing in Publication Data.

A CIP record of this book is available from the British Library.

Author and Series Editor: Shareen Mayers
Commissioning Editor: Shelley Teasdale
Project Manager: Jane Moody
Text Design and Layout: Q2A Media

Inside Concept Design: Ian Wrigley
Cover Design: Anthony Godber
Production: Lyndsey Rogers
Digital Development: www.infuze.co.uk
Printed by Martins the Printers

Contents

Types of words (word classes)	4
Exclamations and exclamation marks	7
Subordinating and coordinating conjunctions	10
Adverbs	13
Prepositions	16
Understanding the past perfect form	19
Direct speech	22
Cohesion within paragraphs	25
Fronted adverbials	28
Apostrophes for contraction and possession	31
Determiners	34
Subordinate clauses and relative clauses	37
Punctuation for parenthesis	40
Active and passive voice	43
Subjunctive verb form	46

Acknowledgements

The author and publisher are grateful to the copyright holders for permission to use quoted material. Every effort has been made to trace copyright holders and obtain their permission for the use of copyright material. The author and publisher will gladly receive information enabling them to rectify any error or omission in subsequent editions.

Auggie and Me, copyright © R. J. Palacio, reproduced by permission of Penguin Random House UK. *Christophe's Story*, copyright © 2007 Nicki Cornwell, reproduced by permission of Frances Lincoln Children's Books. *Fuzzy Mud*, copyright © 2015 Louis Sachar, reproduced by permission of Bloomsbury Publishing plc. *Noughts & Crosses*, copyright © 2002 Malorie Blackman, published by Corgi and reproduced by permission of Bloomsbury Publishing plc. *The Imaginary*, copyright © A. F. Harold, reproduced by permission of Bloomsbury Publishing plc. *The Wreck of the Zanzibar*, copyright © 1995 Michael Morpurgo, reproduced by permission of Egmont UK Ltd. *What's So Special About Shakespeare?* copyright © 2016 Michael Rosen, reproduced by permission of Walker Books Ltd.

Types of words (word classes)

By the end of Year 6, pupils should be able to demonstrate their familiarity with a range of word classes (nouns, verbs, adjectives, conjunctions, pronouns [possessive and relative], adverbs, adverbials, prepositions, determiners and subject and object). Pupils should be able to use the terminology and understand how word classes are used in sentences. This lesson focuses on nouns, verbs, adjectives and pronouns.

Review

- Ask pupils what they understand by the term 'word classes'.
- Remind pupils that word classes make up parts of a sentence and are sometimes called 'parts of speech'.
- Adjectives can be used to modify nouns, to make their meaning more specific. They are sometimes called 'describing words' as they can be used to describe a noun. Verbs can be 'doing' or 'being' words.
- Pronouns can replace a noun; e.g. *she, he, that, which, their*. It is vital that pupils are aware that context is extremely important because words can mean different things depending on the context; for example: 'the *orange* flowers' (adjective) or 'Alfie ate an *orange*' (noun).
- A noun names a person, place, object, feeling or occasion/event. Proper nouns always start with capital letters; e.g. *Sarah Smith*.
- Using the interactive program, ask pupils to drag the missing words into the spaces to make sense of the passage.

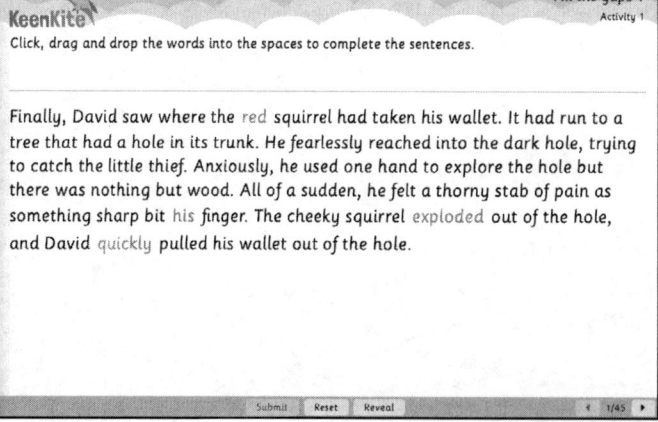

Sentence for modelling

All of a sudden, he felt a thorny stab of pain as something sharp bit <u>his</u> finger.

- In the National Curriculum, pupils need to learn the full range of determiners; for example: *a, an, the, this, that, its, our, their, my, his, her, some, no, every, one, three, four, five*.
- 'His' (in this context) can be both a possessive pronoun and a possessive determiner. If the sentence was: '*My Ferrari was faster than his*', 'his' would be a pronoun because it is not specifying the noun (e.g. '*his Ferrari*').
- Using the interactive program, ask pupils to match the highlighted words to the correct word class.

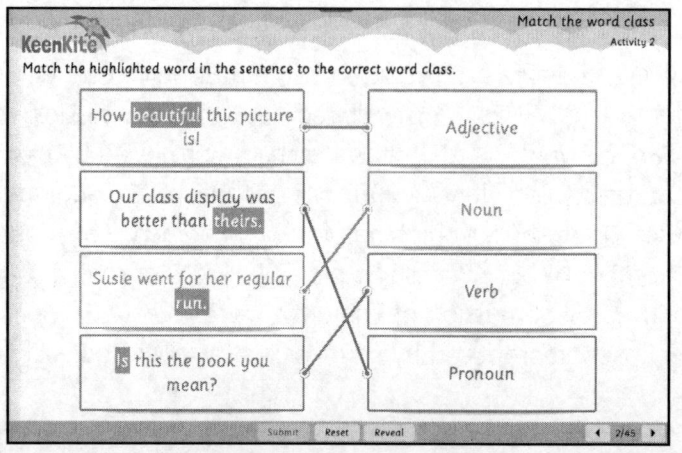

Teach

- Introduce the example text from *The Wreck of the Zanzibar* by Michael Morpurgo (see PDF1).
- Highlight and discuss some of the word classes (e.g. *slipped*, *could* and *followed*) and explain that they are all verbs. 'Could' is a modal verb indicating a degree of possibility.

Practise

- Using the interactive program, ask pupils to identify the word classes used in context.

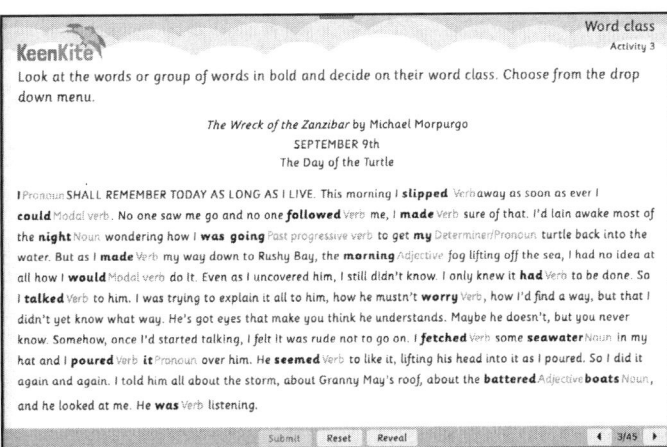

Apply

- Ask pupils to create 'wanted' posters that describe a word class. Ask pupils to select a pronoun, verb, adjective or noun: imagine that one of these word classes has escaped. How would they describe the word class? What could it look like? How is it used?

> **Example:**
>
> **Wanted: the verb**
> Have you seen the verb? It can be used to name an action such as *walked*, *talked* and *followed*. For example, *I walked anxiously across the busy road.* A verb can also be used as a 'being' word: 'is', 'was', 'had' etc. For example, *This book is an adventure story.* They sometimes 'help' other verbs, e.g. 'is going', but not always!

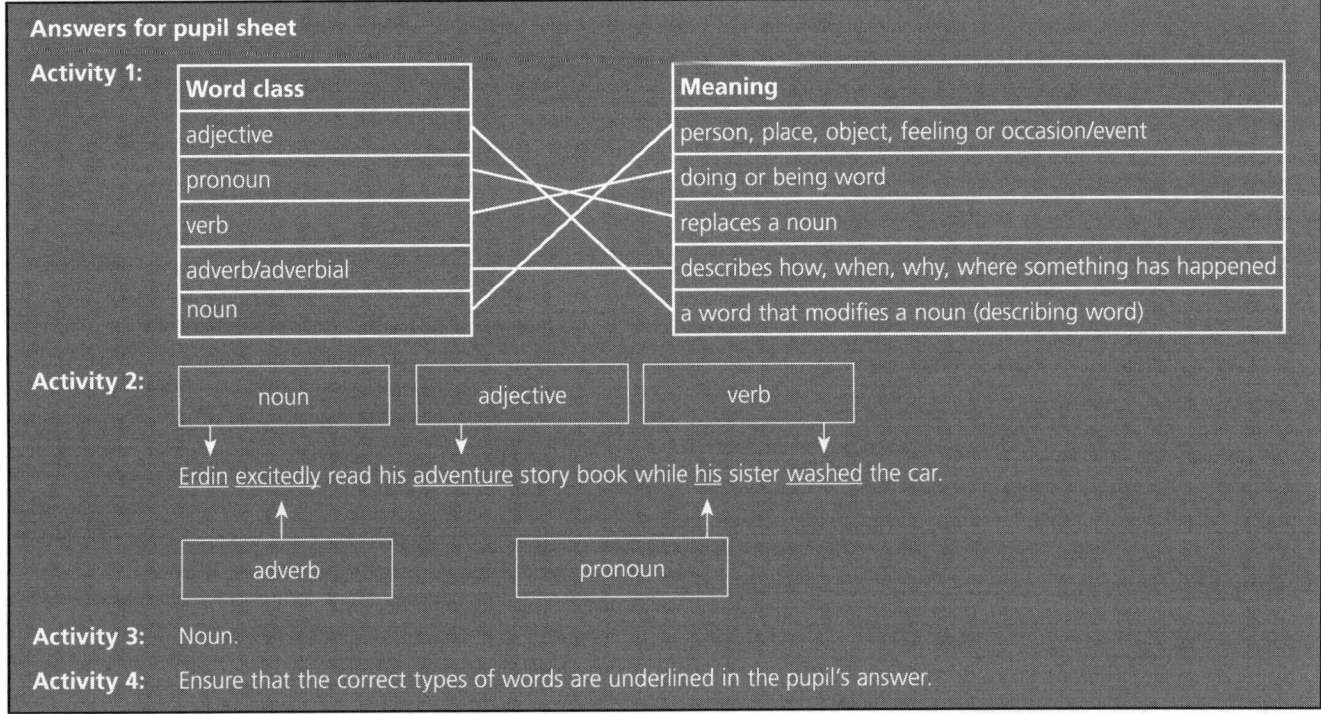

Pupil sheet – Types of words (word classes)

Activity 1

Draw lines to match each word with its simple meaning. The first one has been done for you.

Word class
adjective
pronoun
verb
adverb/adverbial
noun

Meaning
person, place, object, feeling or occasion/event
doing or being word
replaces a noun
describes how, when, why, where something has happened
a word that modifies a noun (describing word)

Activity 2

Write the correct word class from the box in each of the arrow boxes around the sentence. Use each word once. The first one has been done for you.

noun   verb   pronoun   adverb   adjective

noun

Erdin excitedly read his adventure story while his sister washed the car.

Activity 3

What type of word is the word **walk** in the sentence? Tick **one** answer.

*Sara got dressed and went for her **walk**.*

Verb ☐   Pronoun ☐   Preposition ☐   Noun ☐

Activity 4

Now write your own sentences using the word classes below. Underline and identify the type of word in each sentence.

Example:

Types of words: noun, verb   The kangaroo [*noun*] jumped [*verb*].

noun, verb ....

verb, adjective ....

adverb, pronoun ....

Exclamations and exclamation marks

Pupils need to understand the difference between an exclamation mark used for expressing a mood or surprise and an exclamation as a type of sentence. This lesson focuses on the difference between the exclamation mark and the exclamation as a type of sentence.

Review

- Ask pupils to discuss what they think is the difference between an exclamation mark and an exclamation as a type of sentence.
- Remind them that the exclamation mark can be used for any sentence to express a mood, such as heightened emotion.
- The exclamation as a type of sentence starts with 'what' or 'how' and contains a verb.
- Using the interactive program, ask pupils to match the sentences to the correct sentence type.

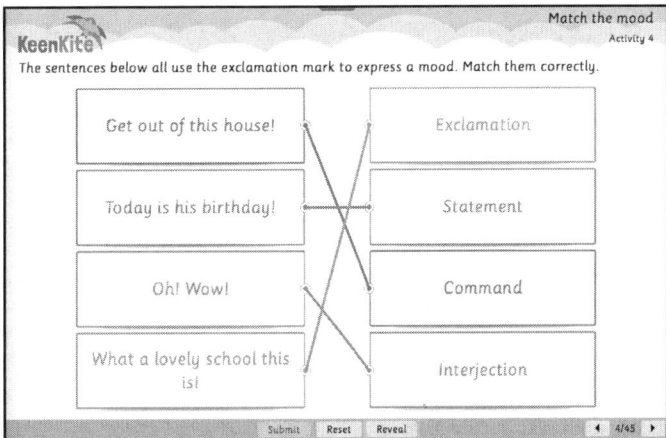

- Using the interactive program, ask pupils to put the words into the correct order in the table to make an exclamation sentence.

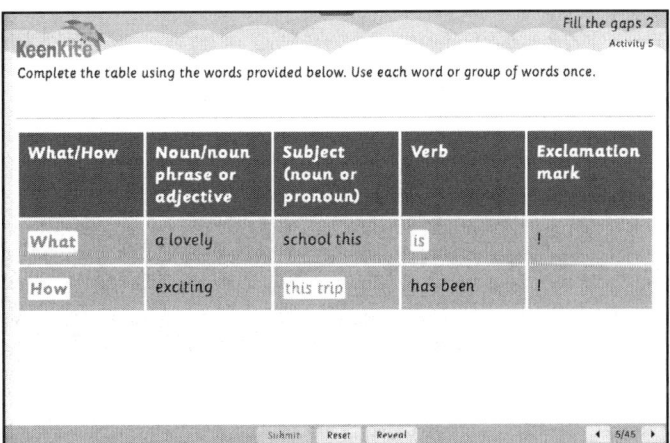

Teach

- Tell pupils that an exclamation sentence is written in a particular way (syntax).
- Ask pupils to discuss and consider what other words would be appropriate for the missing gaps in the table (see interactive program activity 5).
- Display and discuss the table and ask pupils to discuss their own exclamatory sentences using this particular way of grouping words.

Practise

- Introduce the example text from *Christophe's Story* by Nicki Cornwell (see PDF2).
- Using the interactive program, ask pupils to identify whether the sentences in bold are statements or commands.

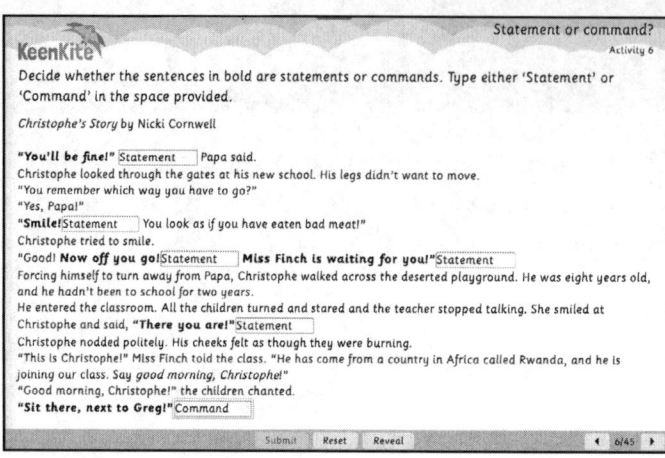

- Ask pupils to identify all the words, phrases or sentences in the extract that use the exclamation mark.

Apply

- Ask pupils to imagine that they are judging a talent contest and they have to give positive and negative feedback using an exclamation sentence. Alternatively, show a clip of an actual talent contest.
- Challenge pupils to create five positive comments and five negative comments in five minutes.
- Ensure that pupils check that they have written an exclamation as a sentence and have not just used the exclamation mark. Consider writing the syntax for an exclamation on the board to remind pupils.

Example:

- *What a talented singer you are!*
- *What an amazing voice you have!*
- *What a great dancer you are!*
- *How superb that performance was!*
- *What an awful performance that was!*
- *How disappointing that was!*

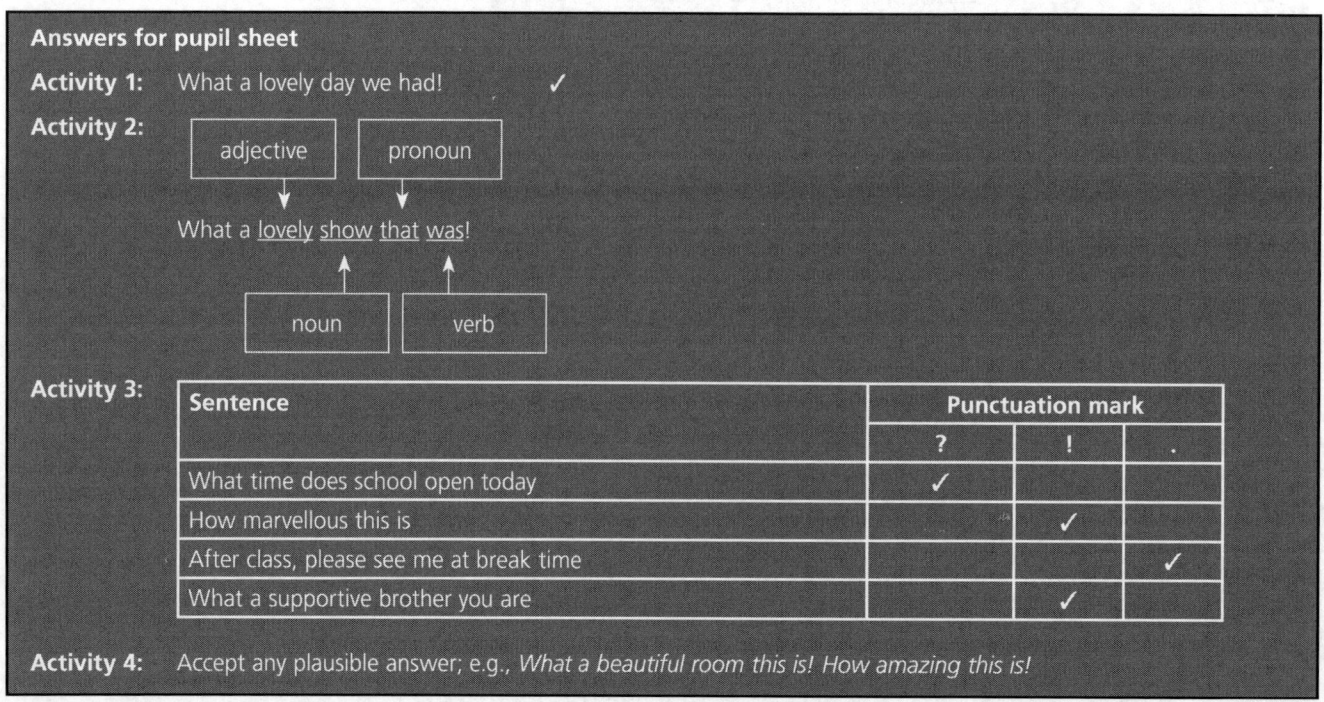

Pupil sheet – Exclamations and exclamation marks

The exclamation mark can be used to express a mood. For example: *Get out of here! I am happy today!*

The exclamation as a type of sentence must start with *What* or *How* and must contain a verb. If there is no verb, then it is called an exclamatory phrase. For example: *How funny!*

Activity 1

Tick the sentence that contains an exclamation as a type of sentence.

Tick **one**

- How exciting!
- What a lovely day we had!
- Oh! Wow!
- What fun!

Activity 2

Label the sentence using the words in the box. Use each word once.

| verb | pronoun | adjective | noun |

What a <u>lovely</u> <u>show</u> <u>that</u> <u>was</u>!

Activity 3

Tick **one** box in each row to show what kind of punctuation mark is needed. Remember the rules for exclamations as a type of sentence. The first one has been done for you.

Sentence	Punctuation mark		
	?	!	.
What time does school open today	✓		
How marvellous this is			
After class, please see me at break time			
What a supportive brother you are			

Activity 4

Imagine that your classroom has been beautifully decorated over the summer holidays. Write an exclamation sentence to describe how you felt and what you saw. Remember to use *What* or *How* and to include a verb.

Subordinating and coordinating conjunctions

Pupils need to be able to distinguish between subordinating and coordinating conjunctions (expressing time, place and cause) and use them to link clauses correctly. Conjunctions are first introduced in Year 3 but this lesson focuses on why certain conjunctions are used.

Review

- Ask pupils to discuss what they think is the difference between a coordinating conjunction and a subordinating conjunction.
- Conjunctions are joining words. A coordinating conjunction can join two words together or it can link phrases and clauses that are of equal importance, such as *and*, *but*, *or*.
- Subordinating conjunctions are used to introduce subordinate clauses; for example *before*, *when*, *because*.

> **Example:**
>
> Time: I bring my umbrella <u>when</u> it is raining/<u>When</u> it is raining, I bring my umbrella.
>
> Place: He hid his money <u>where</u> no one could discover it.
>
> Cause: I brought my raincoat <u>because</u> it was raining.

- The other part of the sentence is called the main clause (e.g. '*He hid his money*' or '*I bring my umbrella*'). The underlined words may also be other types of words, so it is important for pupils to look at how words have been used in context.
- Using the interactive program, ask pupils to identify the correct coordinating conjunctions in the context of the sentence.

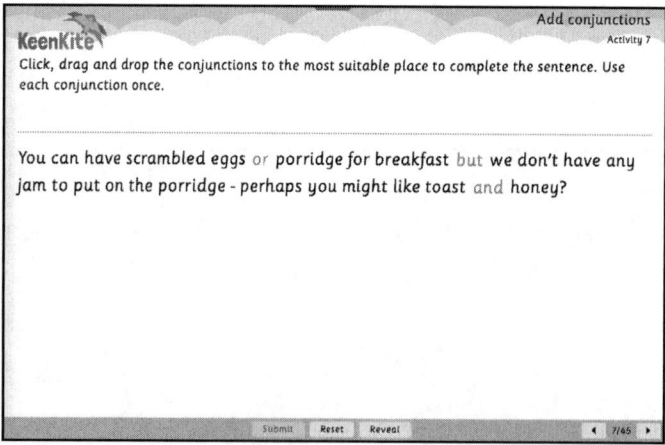

- Using the interactive program, ask pupils to identify the coordinating and subordinating conjunctions. Address any misconceptions during the **Teach** section (page 11).

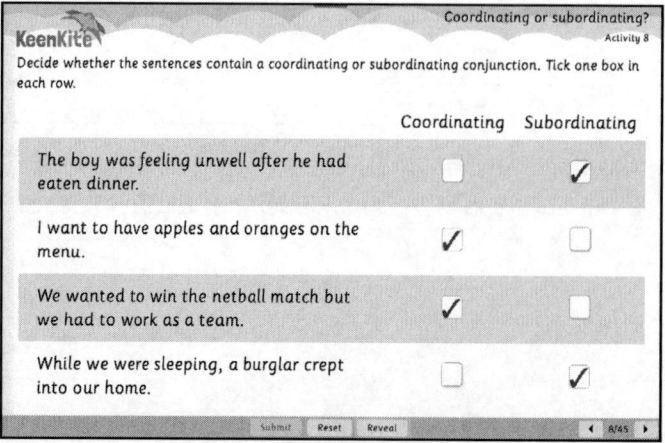

Teach

> **Sentences for modelling**
>
> *The boy was feeling unwell <u>after he had eaten dinner.</u>*
> *<u>While we were sleeping,</u> a burglar crept into our home.*

- Highlight to pupils that the first sentence for modelling is a subordinating conjunction because it introduces a subordinate clause. A subordinate clause tells us extra information within a sentence and contains a verb. In the sentence above, *'had eaten'* is the verb phrase.
- In the second sentence, the subordinate clause is at the start of the sentence. It can be at the beginning or end of the sentence; e.g. *A burglar crept into our home while we were sleeping.* A comma is needed when the subordinate clause is at the start of a sentence. This is also a fronted adverbial but not all fronted adverbials are subordinate clauses; e.g. *After assembly, we got to finish our artwork.* There is no verb in *After assembly*, so it is a fronted adverbial.

Practise

- Introduce the example text: *Complaint email* (see PDF3).
- Using the interactive program, ask pupils to discuss whether the conjunctions in bold and underlined are coordinating or subordinating conjunctions.

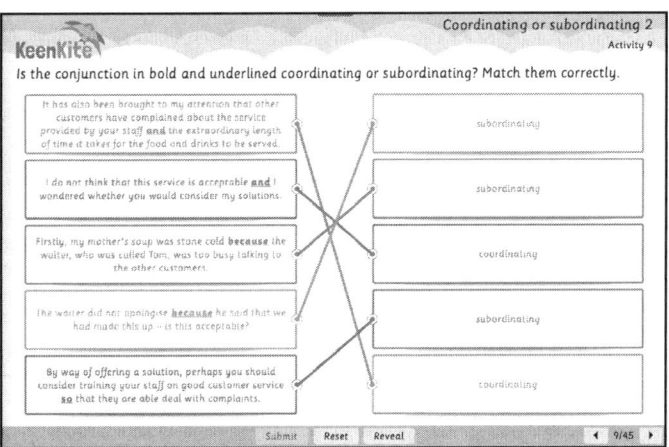

Apply

- Ask pupils to write a reply to the complaint email from the manager of the restaurant.
- Pupils are expected to apply their knowledge of coordinating and subordinating conjunctions.

Answers for pupil sheet			
Activity 1:	Sentence	Subordinating conjunction	Coordinating conjunction
	Please can you bring some pens <u>and</u> a rubber?		✓
	The dog barked <u>when</u> he saw the stranger.	✓	
	<u>Although</u> it was night-time, the street was full of people.	✓	

Activity 2: (Once) Katy had got dressed, she made her way to her friend's house.
(While) crossing the quiet road, he was unaware of the speeding car ahead.

Activity 3: The footballer scored, although the team was playing badly.
The gorilla looked bored, because he wanted to live in the wild.
(Also accept the subordinate clause at the start of the sentence followed by a comma).

Activity 4: Clause used must contain a verb.

Pupil sheet – Subordinating and coordinating conjunctions

Conjunctions are joining words. A coordinating conjunction can join two words together or it can link phrases and clauses that are of equal importance. For example, *and, but, or*.

Subordinating conjunctions are used to introduce subordinate clauses.

Activity 1

Tick **one** box in each row to show whether the underlined word is a subordinating or coordinating conjunction.

Sentence	Subordinating conjunction	Coordinating conjunction
Please can you bring some pens <u>and</u> a rubber?		
The dog barked <u>when</u> he saw the stranger.		
<u>Although</u> it was night-time, the street was full of people.		

Activity 2

Circle all the conjunctions in the sentences below.

Once Katy had got dressed, she made her way to her friend's house.

While crossing the quiet road, he was unaware of the speeding car ahead.

Activity 3

Rewrite these sentences using one of the conjunctions in the box.

| because | although |

Example:

David went up the hill. He was tired.

David went up the hill although he was tired.

The footballer scored. The team was playing badly.

....

The gorilla looked bored. He wanted to live in the wild.

....

Activity 4

Write your own sentence using a subordinating conjunction to introduce a subordinate clause.

....

Adverbs

By the end of Year 6, pupils are expected to be familiar with and know the terminology for a range of word classes, including adverbs. In the Year 3 English programmes of study, pupils are expected to express time, place and cause using adverbs (for example, *then*, *next*, *soon*). Adverbs can modify a verb, an adjective, another adverb or even a whole clause.

Review

- Ask pupils what they understand by the term 'adverb'.
- Explain that adverbs do not always end in –*ly*. They give information relating to *how*, *when*, *how much*, *how often*, *where* or *possibility*.
- Many adverbs also act as cohesive devices which help paragraphs to flow. However, adverbs do not introduce subordinate clauses, as this is the function of a subordinating conjunction.
- Using the interactive program, ask pupils to identify the different types of adverbs and to match them to the underlined words in the sentences.

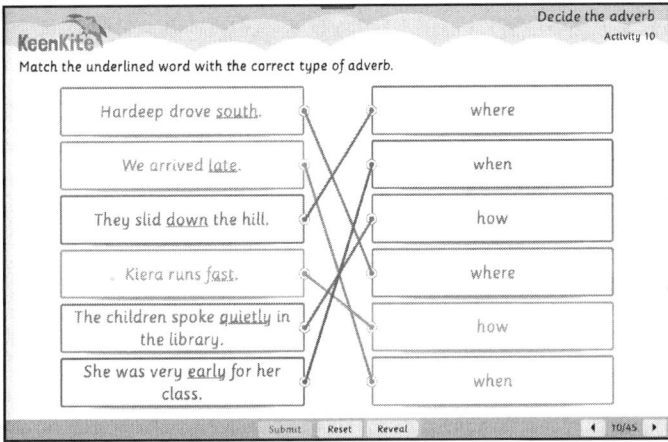

- Using the interactive program, ask pupils to choose the most appropriate adverb for each sentence.

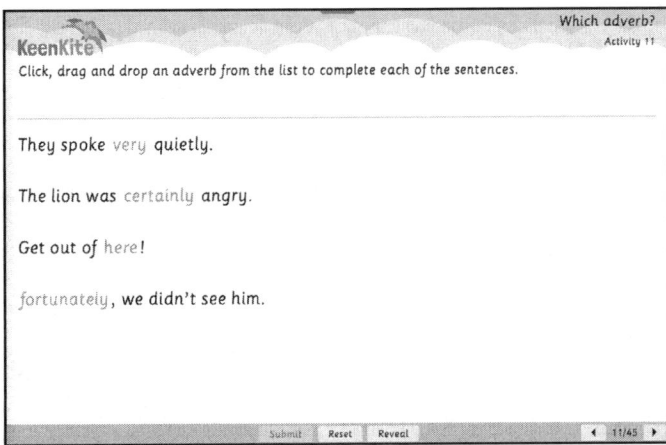

- In the examples shown in interactive activity 11, the adverbs are modifying other word classes, for example, other adverbs, adjectives, nouns and prepositions.

Teach

- Introduce the example text from *Fuzzy Mud* by Louis Sachar (see PDF4).
- Model highlighting the word 'up' in the first sentence and explain that it is an adverb explaining where something has happened.
- Discuss the fact that not all adverbs end in –*ly*.

Practise

- Using the interactive program, ask pupils to decide the type of adverb in the examples within the text.

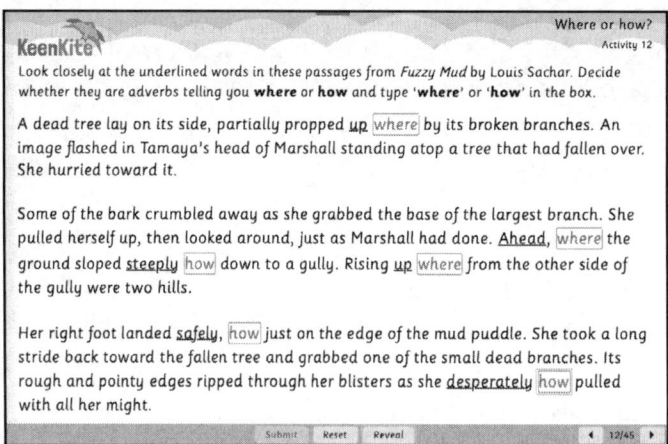

Apply

- Split the class into equal groups. Give each group a key action to perform and an adverb that will be used to describe it.
- Each group should practise their action and the rest of the class must work out the adverb that was used to describe the action. Accept synonyms for words or ask pupils to choose from the verbs and adverbs given below:

| slowly walk | anxiously walk | quickly walk | angrily walk | cautiously walk |

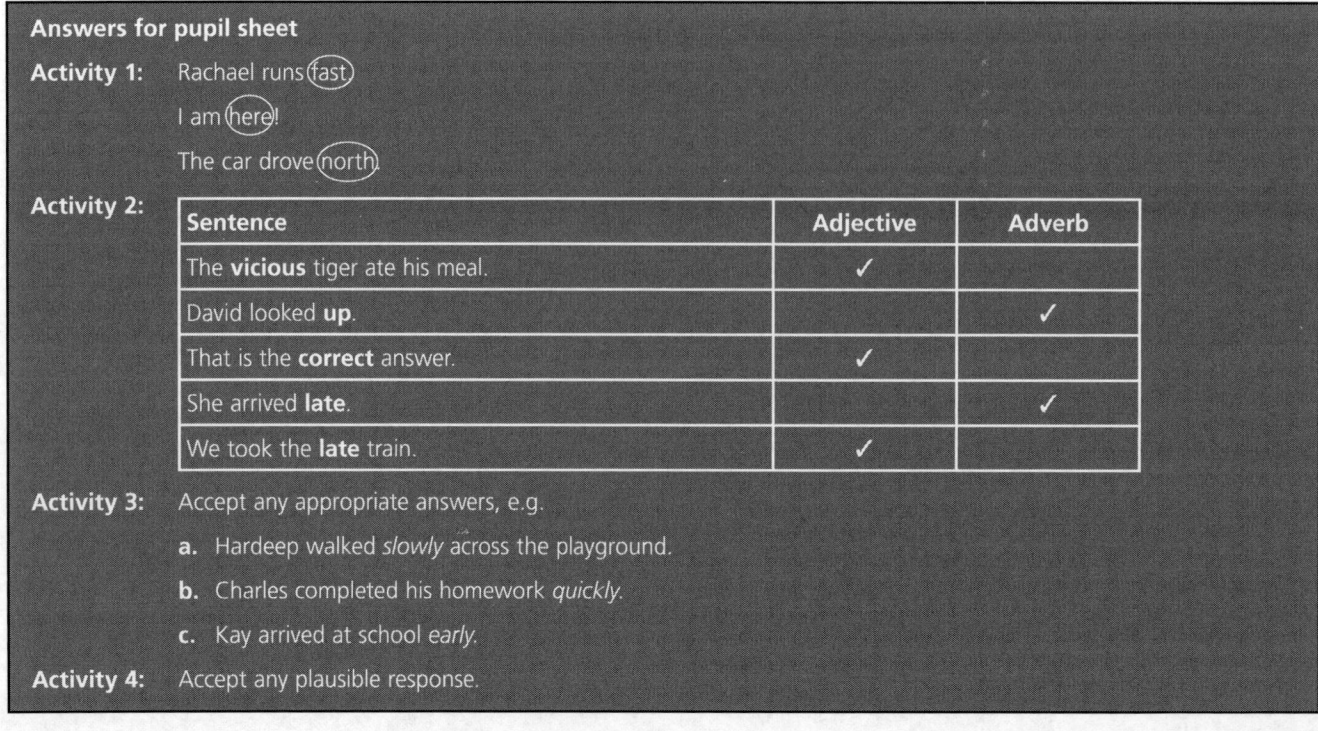

Pupil sheet – Adverbs

Adverbs give us information relating to *how*, *when*, *how much*, *how often*, *where* or *possibility*.

Many adverbs also act as cohesive devices which help paragraphs to flow.

Activity 1

Circle the adverbs in the sentences below.

> **Example:**
> Jamal (slowly) opened the door.

Rachael runs fast.

I am here!

The car drove north.

Activity 2

Tick **one** box in each row to show whether the bold word is an adjective or an adverb. The first one has been done for you.

Sentence	Adjective	Adverb
The **vicious** tiger ate his meal.	✓	
David looked **up**.		
That is the **correct** answer.		
She arrived **late**.		
We took the **late** train.		

Activity 3

Complete each sentence with an appropriate adverb.

a. Hardeep walked _____ across the playground.

b. Charles completed his homework _____ .

c. Kay arrived at school _____ .

Activity 4

Write your own sentence containing an adverb.

_____

_____

Prepositions

By the end of Year 6, pupils are expected to know and understand prepositions of time, place and cause (for example: *before, after, during, in, because of*). Prepositions are first introduced in Year 3 in the English programmes of study. Many prepositions can also be other word classes, so it is important for pupils to be able to identify their function in context; for example, *After 6pm, I visited my friend.* In a different context, 'after' could be used as a subordinating conjunction; for example, *I brushed my teeth after I had eaten.*

Review

- Ask pupils what they understand by the term 'preposition'.
- Explain that prepositions are words that are used before a noun, noun phrase or pronoun to show how things are related or connected to each other. They can describe locations and directions. They can show time, place and cause. For example: place – *in, on, under, below, underneath, near*; time – *after, before, since, until*; cause – *because of*; also movement – *through, into, down, up, on to, to* (show and discuss this with pupils).
- Using the interactive program, ask pupils to identify the prepositions used in the example sentences (pupils will also need to identity the difference between subordinating conjunctions and prepositions).

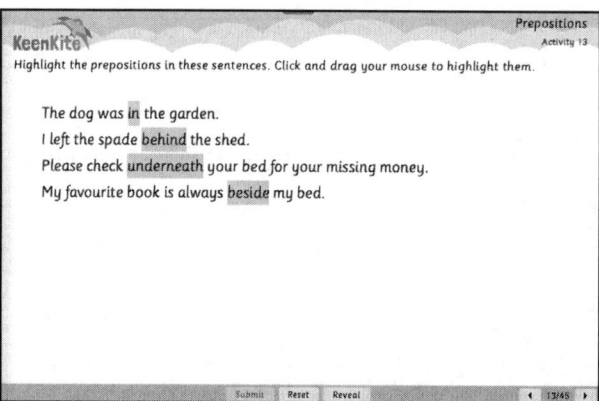

- Using the interactive program, ask pupils to decide whether the underlined words are prepositions or subordinating conjunctions.

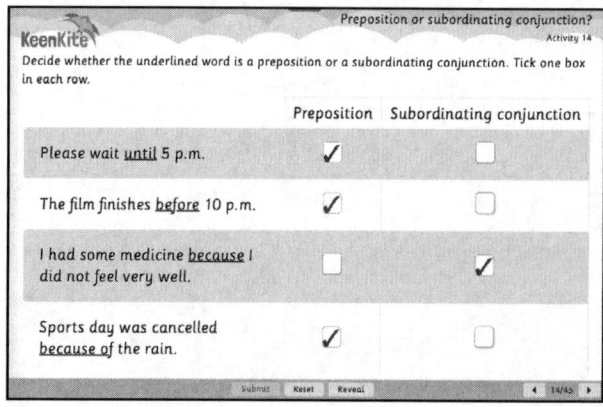

> **Sentence for modelling**
>
> I had some medicine <u>because</u> I did not feel very well.

- Point out to pupils that a subordinating conjunction is used to introduce a subordinate clause. In the example sentence, 'because' introduces the subordinate clause containing a subject (*I*) and verb (*did*). In the example sentence, the person had some medicine *because of* their illness. *Because of* is a preposition of cause; there is no verb.

- In some of the examples in interactive activity 14, the prepositions only show time and are not subordinate clauses because there is no verb.

Teach

- Introduce the example text from *What's So Special About Shakespeare?* by Michael Rosen (see PDF5).
- Model the use of the underlined word 'after' and discuss that it is a preposition of time in this context. Remind pupils that it could also be a subordinating conjunction depending on how it is used within a sentence.

Practise

- Using the interactive program, ask pupils to decide whether the underlined words in the phrases/clauses from the example text (see PDF5) are prepositions of time, place or movement.

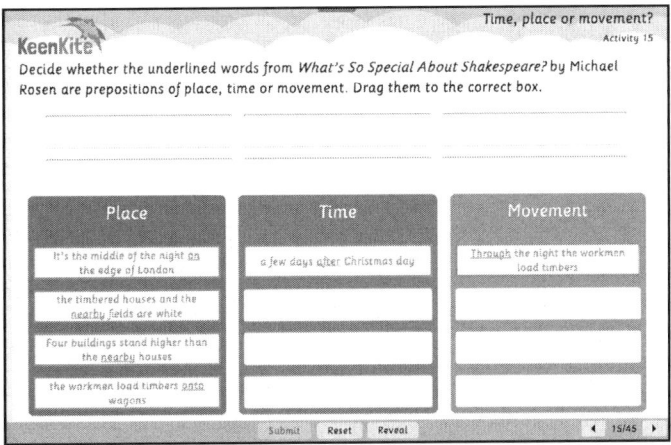

Apply

- Show pupils a range of objects from the classroom: rubber, pencil, paper, books, etc.
- Divide pupils into small groups. Ask each group to hide an object either in the classroom or near the classroom.
- Give pupils a selection of prepositions (under, underneath, over, above, near, on, through, into) and ask them to use some of them to write clear directions so that another group can find the object.
- For example: *The pencil is hidden on the third table along, under the second chair. The rubber is outside in the playground. Find the first bench and look underneath.*

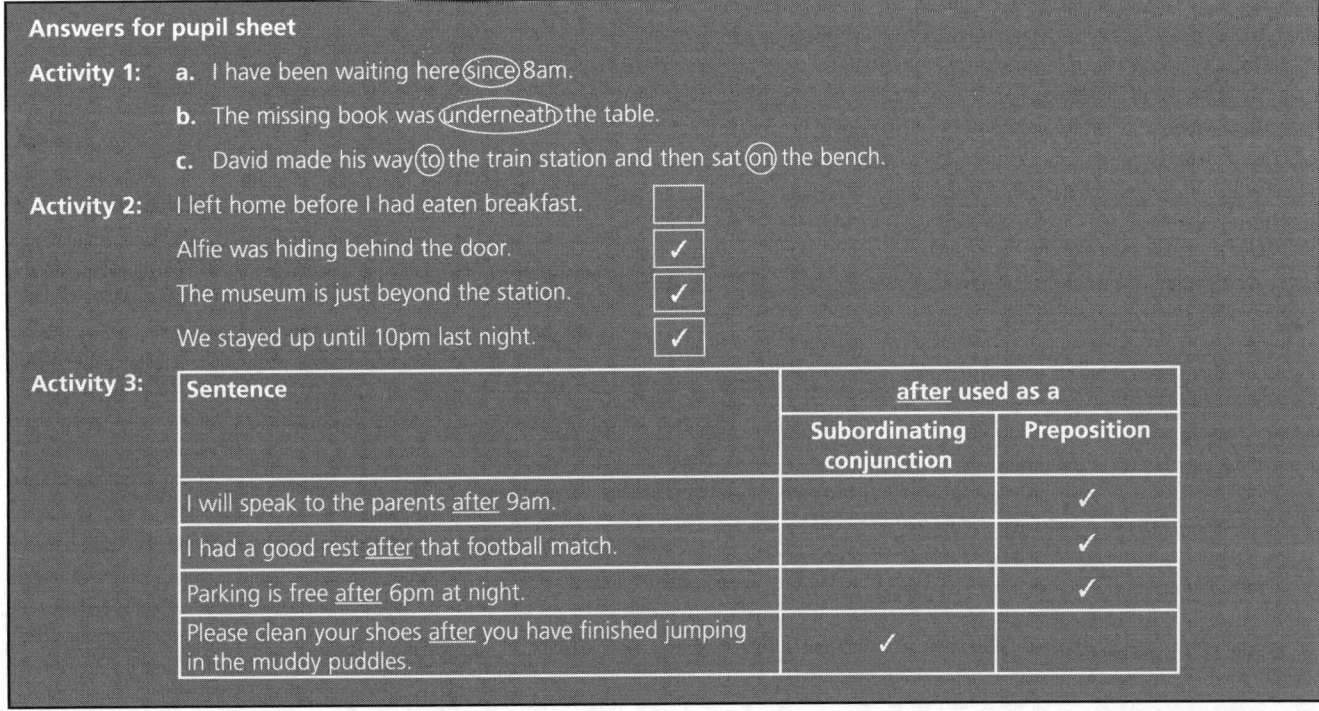

Pupil sheet – Prepositions

Prepositions are words that are used before a noun, noun phrase or pronoun to show how things are related or connected to each other. They can describe locations and directions. For example:

Place – *in, on, under, below, underneath, near*

Time – *after, before, since, until*

Cause – *because of*

Movement – *through, into, down, up, on to, to*

Activity 1

Circle all the prepositions in the sentences.

> **Example:**
> Sara walked anxiously (through) the dark forest and saw a squirrel trying to hide (behind) the tree.

a. I have been waiting here since 8am.

b. The missing book was underneath the table.

c. David made his way to the train station and then sat on the bench.

Activity 2

Tick all the sentences that contain a preposition.

I left home before I had eaten breakfast. ☐

Alfie was hiding behind the door. ☐

The museum is just beyond the station. ☐

We stayed up until 10pm last night. ☐

Activity 3

Tick the box in each row to show whether **after** has been used as a subordinating conjunction to introduce a subordinate clause or as a preposition. Remember: a subordinate clause contains a *subject* and *verb*.

Sentence	after used as a	
	Subordinating conjunction	Preposition
I will speak to the parents <u>after</u> 9am.		
I had a good rest <u>after</u> that football match.		
Parking is free <u>after</u> 6pm at night.		
Please clean your shoes <u>after</u> you have finished jumping in the muddy puddles.		

Understanding the past perfect form

At this stage, pupils should have learnt about consistent tense in Key Stage 1 and will have been taught the present perfect tense in Year 3 (e.g. 'She *has gone* to the shops' instead of 'She *went* to the shops'.) The past perfect tense is mentioned in the Year 5 and Year 6 English programmes of study. Pupils should be able to select and use perfect tense forms. These forms are also used to link ideas across paragraphs (Year 5). This topic focuses on the present perfect form.

Review

- Ask pupils what they understand by past tense verbs.
- Explain to pupils that some verbs talk about events that started in the past but they do not mention the exact time.
- Talk to pupils about this sentence: *They have played tennis four times this week.*
- 'Have played' could mean any time in the past.
- Using the interactive program, ask pupils to complete the sentence using the most appropriate past perfect form of the verb.

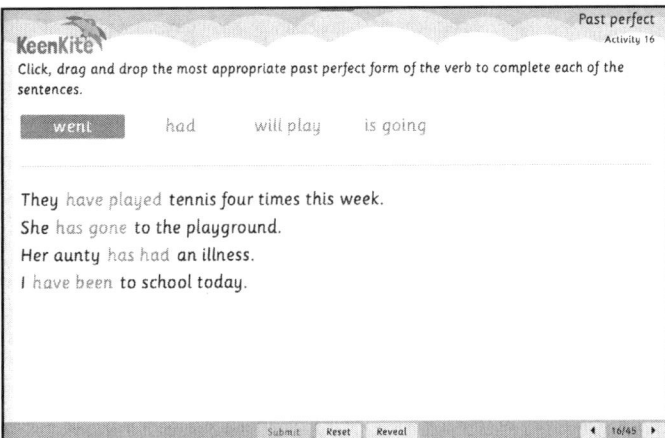

- Using the interactive program, ask pupils to complete the sentences using either *has* or *have*.

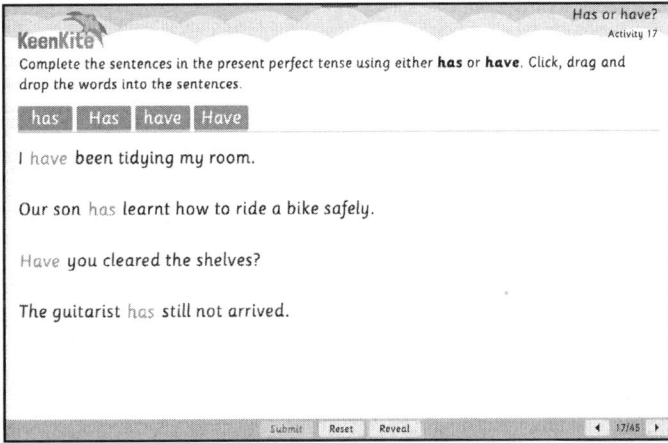

Teach

- Introduce the example text from *Contemporary Narrative: The First Day* (see PDF6).
- Highlight and identify some of the past tense verbs; for example: *thought, remembered, was*.
- Ask pupils to identify some other verbs in the past tense and discuss answers.
- Explain to pupils that the past tense can be written in different ways. This can be explored by using the perfect form of verbs with a particular focus on 'had'.
- Highlight the use of 'had come' and 'had bought' in the example text.
- It is important not to assume that all words ending in –ed are verbs.

Practise

- Using the interactive program, ask pupils to complete the missing past perfect forms.

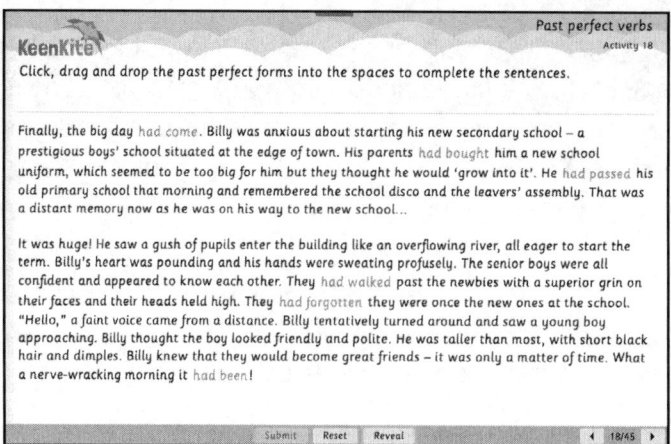

Apply

- Give pupils a verb phrase, such as 'had walked' and ask them to think of as many different ways in which they can write this. Give pupils 30 seconds and then ask them to share ideas with a partner or their table.
- Divide the class into small groups and ask them to practise acting out a particular way of walking. Give each group a sheet or card with their particular action to practise (see ideas below). Once they have practised, each group should present to the class and the rest of the pupils should guess the action.

| **Ideas:** had sprinted | had crept | had trekked | had strolled |

- Pupils can also create a bank of words. For example, 'had walked', 'had strolled', 'had crept', 'had run', 'had sprinted'. These lists can then be used for the pupils' own writing.

Answers for pupil sheet

Activity 1:

Present tense	Simple past tense	Present perfect tense (has or have)	Past perfect tense (had)
look	looked	has/have looked	had looked
catch	caught	has/have caught	had caught
do	did	has/have done	had done
grow	grew	has/have grown	had grown
speak	spoke	has/have spoken	had spoken
hold	held	has/have held	had held

Activity 2:   a. She *had passed* that shop every day for the last two years before she noticed it was empty.

b. The door *had been* left open all night but luckily nothing was missing.

Activity 3:   Accept any plausible answers.

Pupil sheet – Understanding the past perfect from

The past tense can be written using verbs that end in –*ed* or can be formed using irregular verbs.

The present perfect tense is formed by the present tense of 'to have' plus the past participle of the verb.

The past perfect form is formed by the past tense of 'to have' plus the past participle of the verb.

Activity 1

Fill in the missing gaps with the correct answer. The first line has been done for you.

Present tense	Simple past tense	Present perfect tense (has or have)	Past perfect tense (had)
look	looked	has/have looked	had looked
catch			had caught
do	did	has/have done	
grow		has/have grown	had grown
speak		has/have spoken	
hold			

Activity 2

Complete the sentences using the past perfect tense of one of the verbs below. *Remember to check that your sentence makes sense and to use 'had'.*

to pass   **to be**

> **Example:**
> **to buy:** He *had bought* a new car but had to return it later that day.

a. She _____ that shop every day for the last two years before she noticed it was empty.

b. The door _____ left open all night but luckily nothing was missing.

Activity 3

Play the 'Had Been' game. Complete the sentences with an imaginary or real answer.

> **Example:**
> The dragon might not have eaten the man *if he had been more careful.*

a. The BMW might not have crashed if she had been _____

b. The cruise ship might not have sunk if the captain had been _____

c. The tiger might not have attacked the man if he had been _____

d. The snake might not have eaten the rabbit if it had been _____

Direct speech

By the end of Year 6, pupils are expected to use inverted commas (speech marks) to denote speech and to place these correctly in relation to internal punctuation marks. Direct speech is more formally introduced in Years 3 and 4 in the English programmes of study. In Years 5 and 6, pupils are expected to integrate dialogue into their writing where appropriate.

Review

- Ask pupils how they would punctuate direct speech within a piece of writing.
- Remind them that inverted commas (or speech marks) are used to show when people are speaking. In a conversation, you normally have a new line for a new speaker.
- If the information about who is speaking comes before the direct speech, a comma is inserted before the opening inverted commas. The closing inverted commas are inserted after the final punctuation mark. For example: *Sam said, "I will be down in two minutes!"*
- If the information about who is speaking comes after the direct speech, a comma is inserted before the closing inverted commas. For example: *"Let's go swimming," suggested Mia.*
- If the direct speech ends with a question mark or an exclamation mark, the inverted commas still come after the final punctuation mark. For example: *"I can't wait to go on holiday!" exclaimed Freddie.*
- Using the interactive program, ask pupils to correctly punctuate the sentences using the rules for punctuating direct speech.

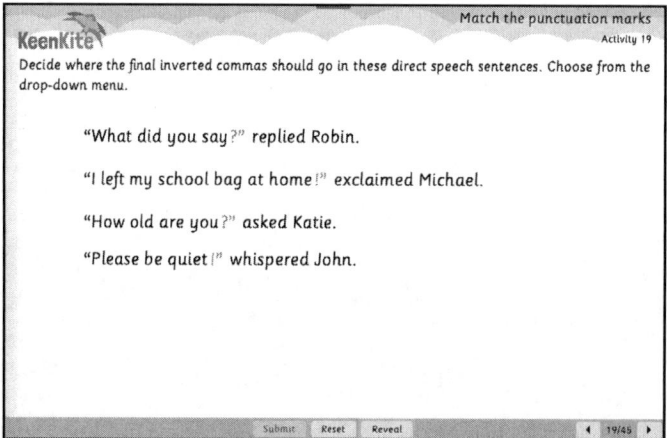

- Using the interactive program, ask pupils to insert the missing commas into the sentences.

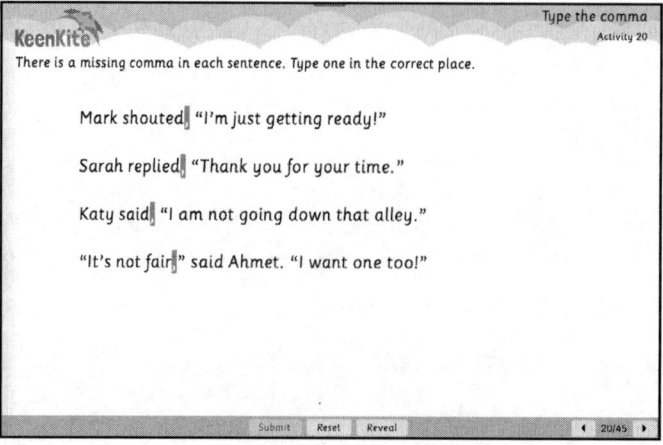

Teach

- Remind pupils that they need a capital letter after the opening inverted commas. Highlight this using the examples in the interactive program.

Practise

- Show pupils the example text from *Auggie and Me* by R. J. Palacio (see PDF7).
- Using the interactive program, model filling in the missing punctuation. Point out that alternative punctuation could also be used in some places; e.g. 'Everyone has!' and 'Yes, he does!' (either exclamation or full stop).

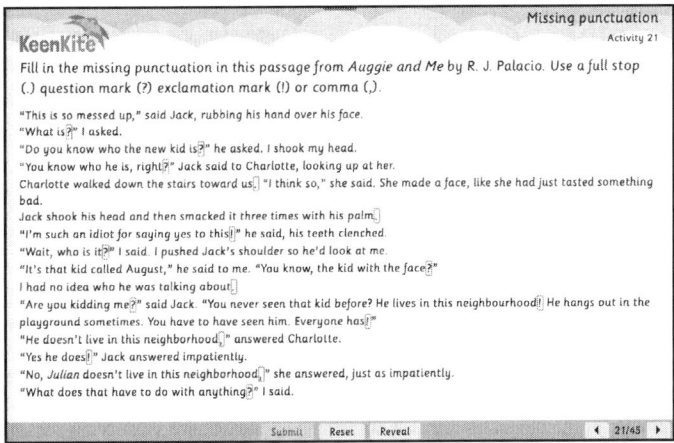

Apply

Give pupils some sentences and ask them to insert the correct punctuation so that they are written as direct speech.

Examples:

Are you coming to my party asked Daniel	→	"Are you coming to my party?" asked Daniel.
I'm really enjoying this song expressed Kim	→	"I'm really enjoying this song!" expressed Kim. (also accept comma)
Can we stay for another hour asked Hardeep	→	"Can we stay for another hour?" asked Hardeep.

Answers for pupil sheet

Activity 1: ✓ ✓

I'm looking forward to watching the football tonight, said Sara.

Activity 2: There should be an exclamation mark after the word 'had'. ✓

There should be an exclamation mark after the closing inverted commas.

The sentence should end with a full stop instead of an exclamation mark. ✓

There should be an exclamation mark after the word 'said'.

More exclamation marks after the word 'Rose' would help to show that they shouted loudly.

Activity 3: He asked her, "Do you want an apple?"

"I have a spare pencil, Hazel," said Uma.

"Harley, shoot at goal!" shouted Anil.

(Accept any other plausible responses.)

Pupil sheet – Direct speech

Inverted commas (or speech marks) are used to show when people are speaking. In a written conversation, you normally start a new line for a new speaker. If the speech starts after the beginning of the sentence, a comma is usually inserted before the inverted commas and punctuation marks are put inside the inverted commas. If the information about who is speaking comes after the direct speech, a comma is inserted before the closing inverted commas.

Activity 1

Tick **two** boxes to show where the missing inverted commas should go.

I'm looking forward to watching the football tonight, said Sara.

Activity 2

You are helping a friend to correct the punctuation in the box. Which **two** pieces of advice should you give to correct the punctuation?

"What a lovely term we've had" said Mrs Rose!

Tick **two**

There should be an exclamation mark after the word 'had'.

There should be an exclamation mark after the closing inverted commas.

The sentence should end with a full stop instead of an exclamation mark.

There should be an exclamation mark after the word 'said'.

More exclamation marks after the word 'Rose' would help to show that they shouted loudly.

Activity 3

Rewrite the sentences below as direct speech using inverted commas. Remember to punctuate them correctly.

He asked her if she wanted an apple.

He asked her, ...

....

Uma told Hazel that she had a spare pencil.

....

....

Anil shouted to Harley to shoot at goal.

....

....

Cohesion within paragraphs

By the end of Year 6, pupils are expected to link ideas across paragraphs using a wider range of cohesive devices to help their paragraphs to flow. These could include repetition of a word or phrase, the use of adverbials such as *'on the other hand'*, *'in contrast'* or *'as a consequence'*, and ellipsis.

Review

- Ask pupils what they understand by the term 'cohesion'.
- Explain that cohesive devices, such as adverbs and adverbials, help paragraphs to flow.
- Explain that adverbs do not always end in *–ly*. They give information relating to *how, when, how much, how often, where, possibility*.
- Explain that an adverbial is a word (adverb) or groups of words (phrase/clause) that tells how (manner), when (time), where (place), why, how often (frequency) or number (first, secondly, once, twice).
- Adverbials can also link to what has happened before; for example, *on the other hand, in contrast, in addition, however, despite this, subsequently*.
- An adverbial does not always need to be at the start of a sentence.
- See also the section on **Fronted adverbials** (pages 28–29) for further examples and explanation.
- Using the interactive program, ask pupils to choose the most appropriate adverbial to complete the sentences.

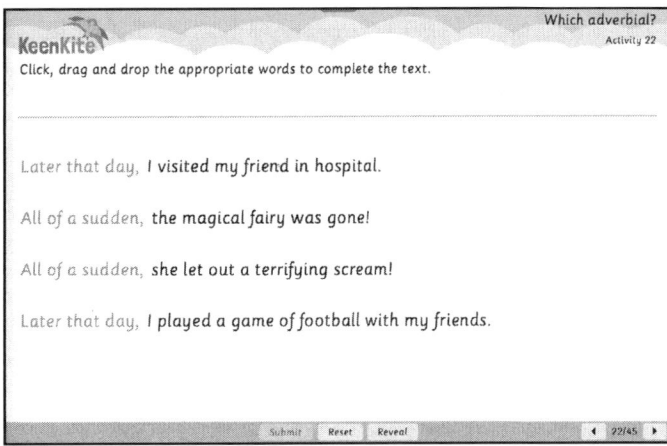

- Using the interactive program, ask pupils to complete the text.

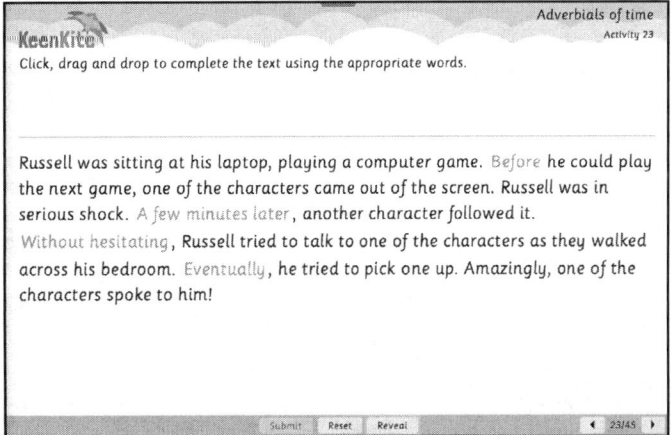

Teach

- Explain to pupils that, within a paragraph, we normally have a topic sentence, which explains or introduces what a paragraph is about.

- In the interactive program, 'Russell was sitting at his laptop, playing a computer game.' is the topic sentence and the rest of the paragraph gives us details about what happened when he was sitting at his laptop. This text is often called 'supporting details'. Within the paragraph, words like, 'Before', 'A few minutes later', 'Without hesitating' and 'Eventually,' all help to move the paragraph along and support the flow of the paragraph.

Practise

- Using the example text – letter of application for the football team (see PDF8) – model identifying the cohesive devices that help the paragraphs to flow.

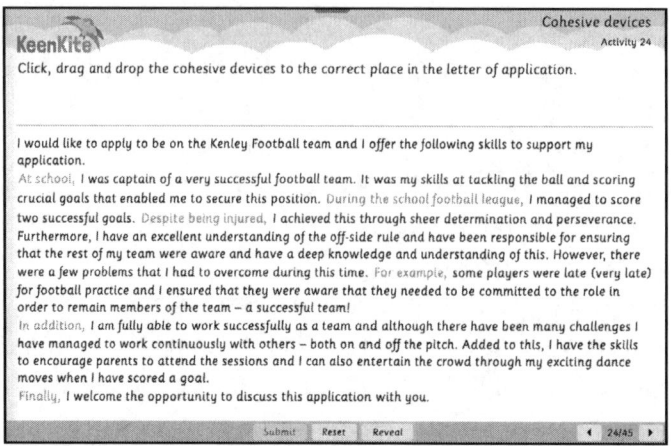

Apply

- Ask pupils to rewrite the example text to use a greater variety of fronted adverbials and language that will persuade the reader to give the applicant a place on the team.
- Ask pupils to edit and proof-read their writing, paying attention to the grammar that they have used and considering any grammar areas that have previously been taught.
- Remind pupils that editing involves making changes to grammar and vocabulary to improve the text. Proof-reading focuses on checking spelling and punctuation.

Answers for pupil sheet

Activity 1:
a. <u>Firstly</u>, sweets are not good for your teeth.
b. <u>Despite the delay</u>, they still made it to Spain.
c. <u>Finally</u>, we reached our destination.

Activity 2:
As a noun phrase
As an adverb ✓
As a subordinate clause
As a main clause

Activity 3:

Sentence	Adverb used correctly	Adverb used incorrectly
It didn't fortunately rain.		✓
Secondly, it is unhealthy for your teeth.	✓	
Therefore, please wipe your feet when you enter.	✓	
I made finally my way to the beach.		✓

Pupil sheet – Cohesion within paragraphs

Cohesive devices, such as adverbs and adverbials, help paragraphs to flow. They give information relating to *how, when, how much, how often, where, possibility*. Adverbs do not always end in *–ly*.

An adverbial is a word (adverb) or groups of words (phrase/clause) that tells how (manner), when (time), where (place), why, how often (frequency) or number (first, secondly, once, twice).

Adverbials can also link to what has happened before. For example, *on the other hand, in contrast, in addition, however, despite this, subsequently*.

Activity 1

Underline the fronted adverbials in the sentences below.

Example:

All of a sudden, it began to rain.

a. Firstly, sweets are not good for your teeth.

b. Despite the delay, they still made it to Spain.

c. Finally, we reached our destination.

Activity 2

Tick the option which shows how the underlined word in the sentence below is used.

Furthermore, there are dangerous flying creatures in that cave.

	Tick **one**
As a noun phrase	☐
As an adverb	☐
As a subordinate clause	☐
As a main clause	☐

Activity 3

Decide whether the adverb has been used correctly in each sentence. Tick **one** box in each row.

The first one has been done for you.

Sentence	Adverb used correctly	Adverb used incorrectly
It didn't fortunately rain.		✓
Secondly, it is unhealthy for your teeth.		
Therefore, please wipe your feet when you enter.		
I made finally my way to the beach.		

Fronted adverbials

By the end of Year 6, pupils need to be able to identify and use adverbials and fronted adverbials to show time and place (for example, *Later that morning, I met my friend*). Adverbials are introduced in Year 4, when pupils are expected to learn how to use a comma after a fronted adverbial. This lesson focuses on using fronted adverbials.

Review

- Ask pupils to discuss what they understand by the term 'adverbial'.
- Explain that an adverbial is a word (adverb) or groups of words (phrase/clause) that modifies a verb, an adjective, another adverb or clause. It can tell how (manner), when (time), where (place), why, how often (frequency) or number (first, secondly, once, twice).
- If you asked the question *when? where? how? why?* or *how often?* most adverbials would answer this question.
- Adverbials can also link to what has happened before; for example, *on the other hand, in contrast, in addition, however, despite this, subsequently*.
- An adverbial can be at the beginning, middle or end of a sentence.
- Using the interactive program, ask pupils to identify the different types of adverbials.

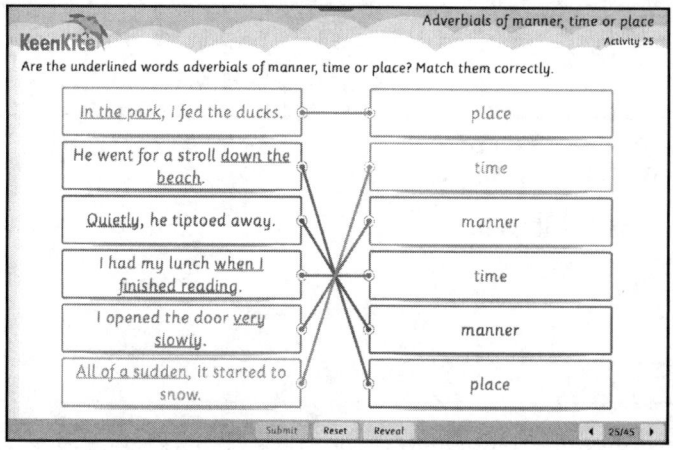

> **Sentences for modelling**
>
> *In the park*, I fed the ducks.
> I had my lunch *when I finished reading*.

- Explain to pupils that an adverbial is an umbrella term for a range of things. Adverbials can be an adverb (word), an adverb phrase, a prepositional phrase or a subordinate clause.
- In the first sentence, '*In the park*' is also a prepositional phrase. In the second sentence, '*when I finished reading*' is also a subordinate clause containing the verb 'finished'.

Teach

- Adverbials can help paragraphs to flow (cohesion).
- Introduce the example text – *Discussion: Should pupils bring mobile phones to school?* (see PDF9) – and model finding the first fronted adverbial, '*Over the past decade*'.
- Using the interactive program, ask pupils to choose the most appropriate fronted adverbial for the sentence.

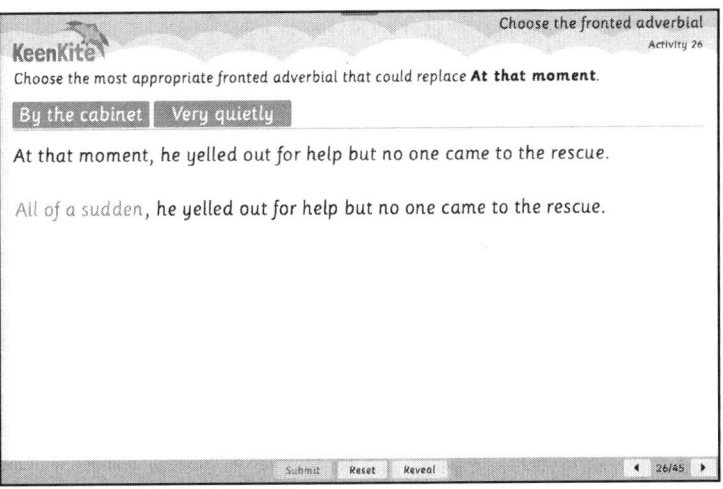

Practise

- Using the interactive program, show pupils the example text and ask them to place the fronted adverbials in the most appropriate place in the text.

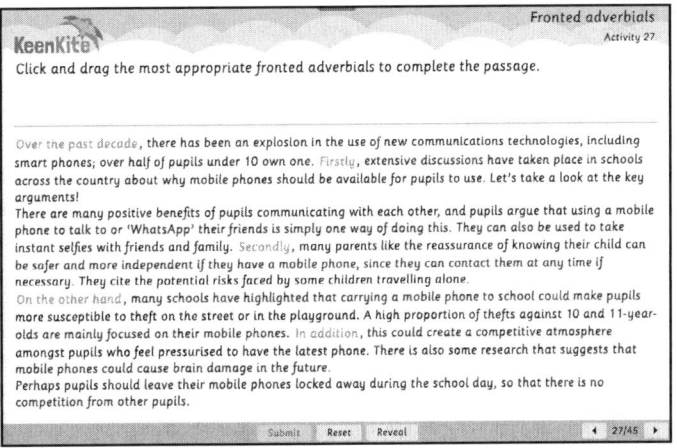

Apply

- Discuss with pupils whether they think they should be allowed mobile phones in school.
- Imagine that they have been given the chance to present their arguments to the head teacher/principal. Ask pupils to write a short speech of no more than five lines, stating why they think they should or should not have mobile phones in school.
- Remind pupils to apply their knowledge of adverbials or fronted adverbials in their speech. For example: Firstly, *I think that we should have mobile phones because they keep pupils safe when walking to school. Secondly, they have useful educational apps on them which can help with learning. Finally, they do not have to be in class and can be locked away during the day.*

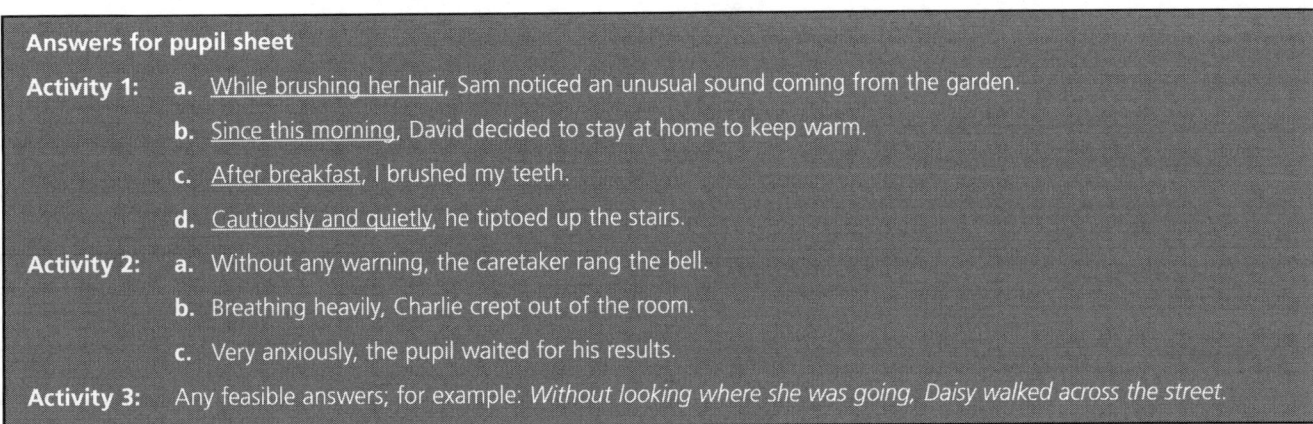

Pupil sheet – Fronted adverbials

An adverbial is a word (adverb) or groups of words (phrase/clause) that tells how (manner), when (time), where (place), why, how often (frequency) or number (first, secondly, once, twice).

Fronted adverbials are placed at the start of sentences followed by a comma.

Activity 1

Underline all the fronted adverbials used in the sentences below.

Example:

Once a week, Sarah went to the gym.

a. While brushing her hair, Sam noticed an unusual sound coming from the garden.

b. Since this morning, David decided to stay at home to keep warm.

c. After breakfast, I brushed my teeth.

d. Cautiously and quietly, he tiptoed up the stairs.

Activity 2

Change these sentences so that the adverbial is at the front.

Example:

You will not feel the pain after a while.   After a while, you will not feel the pain.

a. The caretaker rang the bell without any warning.

b. Charlie crept out of the room breathing heavily.

c. The pupil waited for his results very anxiously.

Activity 3

Complete this sentence with a fronted adverbial of your choice. Remember to use a comma.

.... Daisy walked across the street.

Apostrophes for contraction and possession

By the end of Year 6, pupils are expected to identify, form and expand contractions accurately. They are also expected to use apostrophes correctly for omission and singular possession, and mostly accurately for plural possession. Apostrophes for contractions and singular possession are first introduced in Year 2 and apostrophes for plural possession are first introduced in Year 4.

Review

- Ask pupils what they understand by the term 'apostrophe of contraction'.
- Explain that the apostrophe can be used to show when a letter or letters have been taken out of a word. If you want to write 'could not' in its contracted form, you remove the 'o' from *not* and join the words together: *couldn't*. The apostrophe is placed exactly above where the missing letter or letters would be.
- Apostrophes for possession are used to show when something belongs to someone or something. For example, *the coat belonging to the girl* becomes *the girl's coat*.
- If there is more than one girl, then the apostrophe is placed after the plural form: *the girls' coats*.
- Using the interactive program, ask pupils to match the contractions to their expanded form.

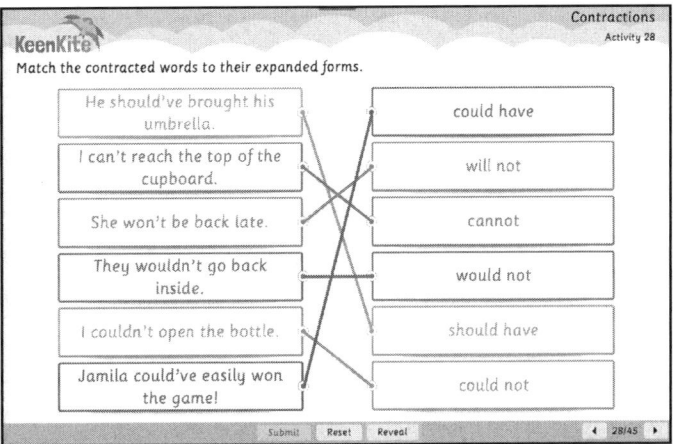

- Remind pupils that *should've* and *could've* are short for *should have* and *could have* and not 'of'!
- Using the interactive program, ask pupils to decide whether the apostrophes are used for contraction or possession.

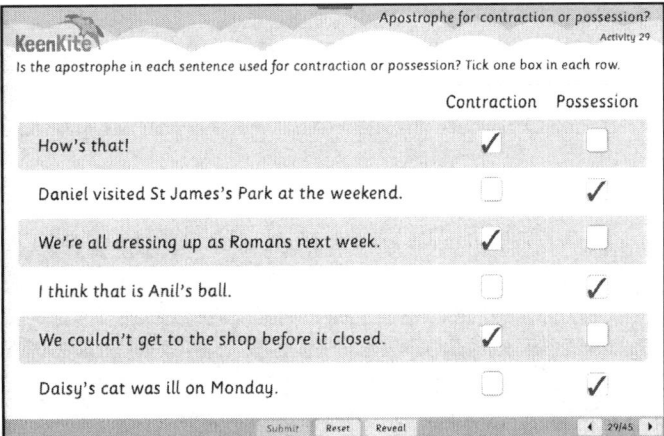

> **Sentence for modelling**
>
> Daniel visited St James's Park at the weekend.

- According to the English programme of study in the Year 3 and Year 4 spelling appendix, if a plural noun ends in 's' the 's' suffix is required, e.g. *Cyprus's population* or *Chris's book*.

31

Teach

- Introduce the example text from *The Imaginary* by A. F. Harold (see PDF10).
- Model changing the word 'can't' back to its expanded form, *cannot*.
- Review and discuss the letters that have been omitted.

Practise

- Using the interactive program, ask pupils to find the contractions in the text and replace them with the expanded form.

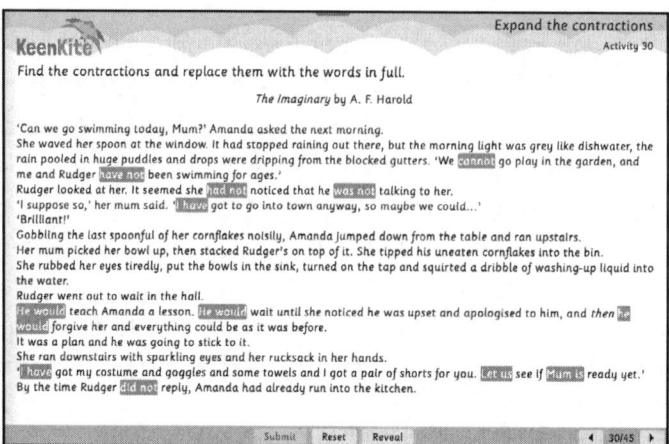

- The contraction 'ain't' has been expanded for completeness. Point out that it is non-Standard English.

Apply

- Use the text below to create three posters.
- Ask pupils to look at the poster text. Each one has errors. Ask pupils to correct the errors with the correct use of apostrophes.

Example:

Poster 1: Apple's, orange's and pear's for sale here!   (Apples, oranges and pears for sale here!)
Poster 2: Welcome to the childrens' area!   (Welcome to the children's area!)
Poster 3: Customer's for taxi's, please turn left.   (Customers for taxis, please turn left.)

- Optional: Look at the song lyrics of some of the pupils' favourite pop songs. Ask them to change the contracted forms to their expanded forms.

Answers for pupil sheet

Activity 1:
    a. <u>I am</u> visiting Grandma later, but I <u>will not</u> be back late.
    b. Please <u>do not</u> wait up for me.
    c. I <u>cannot</u> do that – <u>it is</u> too difficult.

Activity 2: We're going to (Sarah's) house at 6 o'clock so make sure you are on time as Ben's going out at 8 o'clock.

Activity 3: <u>It has</u> been a long day and <u>I have</u> still got homework to do for the morning. I <u>cannot</u> wait to get home so I can make a start. I <u>should have</u> started it yesterday!

Activity 4:

Sentence	Contraction	Possession
Tom's cat Fluffy fell in the fishpond.		✓
Fluffy couldn't get out by herself.	✓	
Tom ran to get his mum's help.		✓

Pupil sheet – Apostrophes for contraction and possession

The apostrophe can be used to show when a letter or letters have been taken out of a word. If you want to write 'could not' in its contracted form, you remove the 'o' and join the words together: *couldn't*. The apostrophe is placed directly above where the missing letter or letters would be.

Apostrophes for possession are used to show when something belongs to someone or something. For example, *the coat belonging to the girl* becomes *the girl's coat*. If there is more than one girl, then the apostrophe is placed after the plural form: *the girls' coats*.

Activity 1

Replace the underlined words in the sentence below with their expanded forms.

a. <u>I'm</u> visiting Grandma later, but I <u>won't</u> be back late.

b. Please <u>don't</u> wait up for me.

c. I <u>can't</u> do that – <u>it's</u> too difficult.

Activity 2

Circle one word in the passage that contains an apostrophe for possession.

We're going to Sarah's house at 6 o'clock so make sure you are on time as Ben's going out at 8 o'clock.

Activity 3

Rewrite the sentence below by changing all the underlined words to their expanded form.

<u>It's</u> been a long day and <u>I've</u> still got homework to do for the morning. I <u>can't</u> wait to get home so I can make a start. I <u>should've</u> started it yesterday!

Activity 4

Decide whether the apostrophes in these groups of words are being used for contraction or possession. Add a tick in the correct box.

Sentence	Contraction	Possession
Tom's cat Fluffy fell in the fishpond.		
Fluffy couldn't get out by herself.		
Tom ran to get his mum's help.		

Determiners

By the end of Year 6, pupils need to be familiar with a wide range of word classes. They need to use the terminology and understand how they are used in sentences. Determiners are first introduced in Year 4 in the English programmes of study.

Review

- Ask pupils what they understand by the term 'determiner'. The term 'determiner' is an umbrella term for a range of different determiners. Pupils do not need to know the sub-terms but it may help to differentiate between them:
  - determiners specify a noun
  - articles: *the*, *a*, *an*
  - demonstratives: *this*, *that*, *these*, *those*
  - possessives: *its*, *our*, *their*, *my*, *your*, *his*, *her*
  - quantifiers: *some*, *all*, *enough*, *both*, *little*, *many*, *either*, *every*, *other*, *another*, *any*, *much*, *no*
  - numerals: *one* (1), *two* (2), *three* (3), *four* (4).
- It is important to recognise that some determiners can also act as pronouns. For example, 'his' can be both a possessive pronoun and a possessive determiner: *My Ferrari is faster than his*, where 'his' is a pronoun because it is not specifying the noun: *My Ferrari is faster than his Ferrari*, where 'his' is a possessive determiner. For further details on **Pronouns** see pages 4–5.
- Using the interactive program, ask pupils to identify all of the determiners used in the sentences.

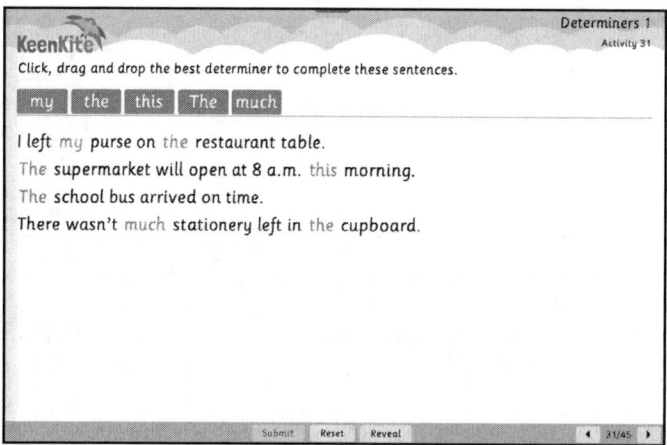

- Discuss with pupils that 'a' comes before a word beginning with a consonant and 'an' comes before a word beginning with a vowel. There are some exceptions to this rule, such as 'eu' and 'u' when they make the 'y' sound (for example, 'a European passport', 'a unicorn') and words which start with a silent 'h', such as 'an hour'.
- Using the interactive program, ask pupils to insert 'a' or 'an' in front of the words given.

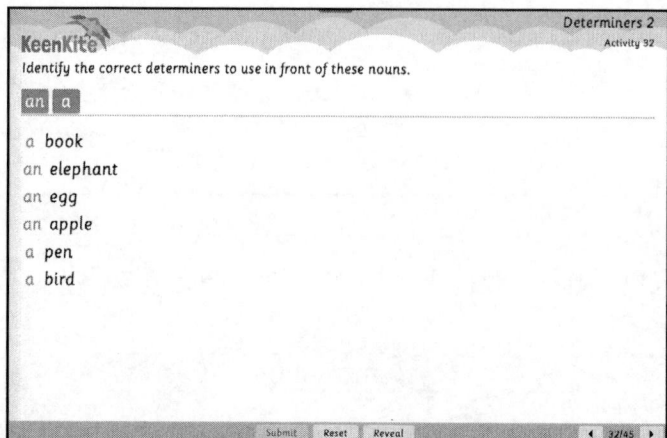

34

Teach

- Introduce the example text from *Noughts and Crosses* by Malorie Blackman (see PDF11).
- Model finding the determiner with the first example, 'her eyes'. Highlight the fact that the word 'her' is specifying whose eyes.
- Ask pupils to identify examples of determiners.

Practise

- Using the interactive program, ask pupils to choose the determiners that are used to specify the nouns.

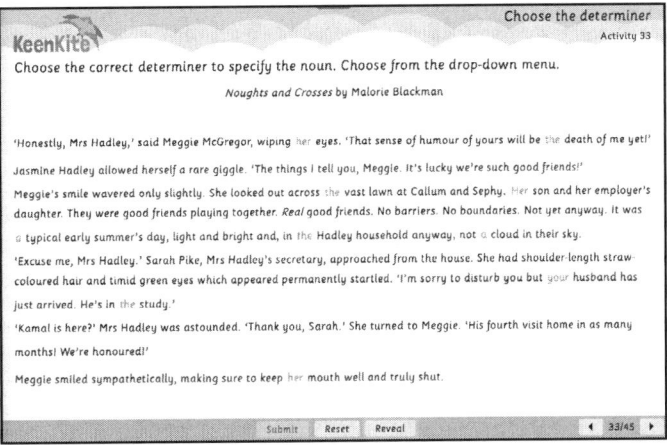

Apply

- Divide the class into small groups or tables.
- Select a range of objects from across the classroom, such as pens, paper, scissors, whiteboards, books.
- Assign an object to each group and give them some paper to record their answers.
- Give each group 30 seconds to think of as many determiners that they can use to describe their object.
- The group with the most determiners is the winner.

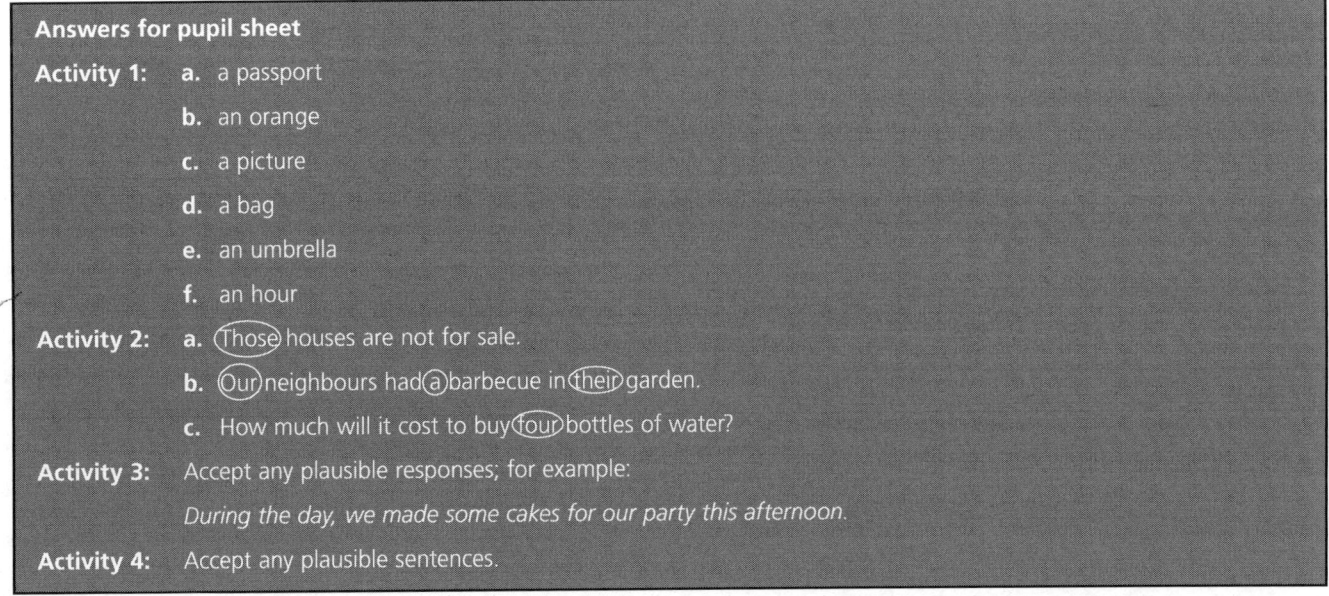

35

Pupil sheet – Determiners

A determiner is a word or group of words that specify or introduce a noun. They add context to the noun. The noun may be known (*the book*) or unknown (*a book*). Determiners can also tell you how much (*a few sweets*) or who owns something (*her coat*).

Activity 1

Write either **a** or **an** in front of these nouns.

a. .... passport

b. .... orange

c. .... picture

d. .... bag

e. .... umbrella

f. .... hour

Activity 2

Circle all the determiners in the sentences below.

> **Example:**
>
> "I don't have (much) money today but I can pay you on Friday."

a. Those houses are not for sale.

b. Our neighbours had a barbecue in their garden.

c. How much will it cost to buy four bottles of water?

Activity 3

Fill in the missing gaps with an appropriate determiner.

During .... day, we made .... cakes for .... party .... afternoon.

Activity 4

Write your own sentence containing at least **two** determiners. Underline the determiners you have used.

....

....

Subordinate clauses and relative clauses

By the end of Year 6, pupils need to be able to identify and use main clauses and subordinate clauses (including relative clauses) in a sentence. Subordinate clauses are first introduced in Years 2 and 3. Relative clauses are first introduced in Year 5.

Review

- Using the interactive program, ask pupils to independently complete the answers.

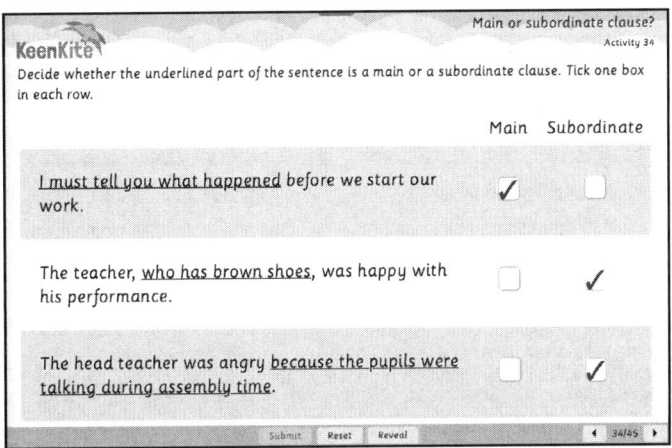

> **Sentences for modelling**
>
> Mrs Jones was pleased <u>because everyone liked her cakes</u>.
> The walker, <u>who had blisters</u>, was limping home.

- Show pupils the two sentences above and ask them to identify the main and subordinate clause.
- What do most clauses have? They mainly have a subject (noun/proper noun/pronoun) and a verb.
- Identify the subject and verbs: the pupils (subject), were talking (verb)/who (pronoun), has (verb). In the second sentence, also identify the relative clause.
- A subordinate clause provides extra information within a sentence. It would not make sense on its own: it is not a complete sentence. A subordinating conjunction is used to introduce a subordinate clause.
- A relative clause is a special type of subordinate clause introduced by a relative pronoun. In general, use *who*, *whom*, and *whose* for people and *which* and *that* for non-human subjects. 'Subordinate clause' is the umbrella term.
- The relative pronoun can also be omitted within a sentence. For example, *This is the car that I told you about./This is the car I told you about.*
- A subordinating conjunction is used to introduce a subordinate clause.
- Using the interactive program, ask pupils to identify the most appropriate option to introduce the subordinate clause.

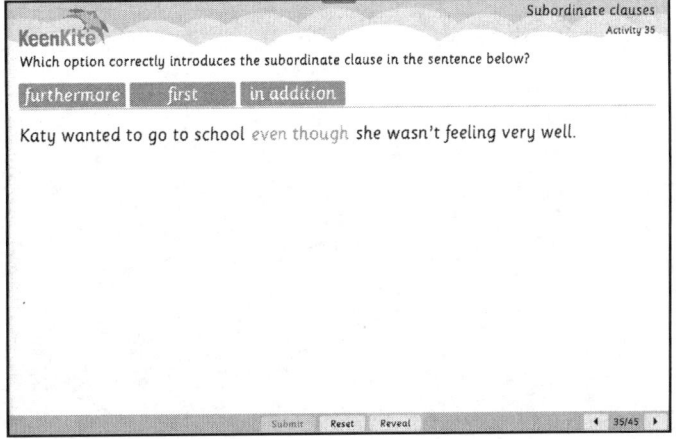

Teach

- Introduce pupils to the example text *Spooky House* (see PDF12).
- Using the interactive program, ask pupils to identify the main and subordinate clauses used in the example text.

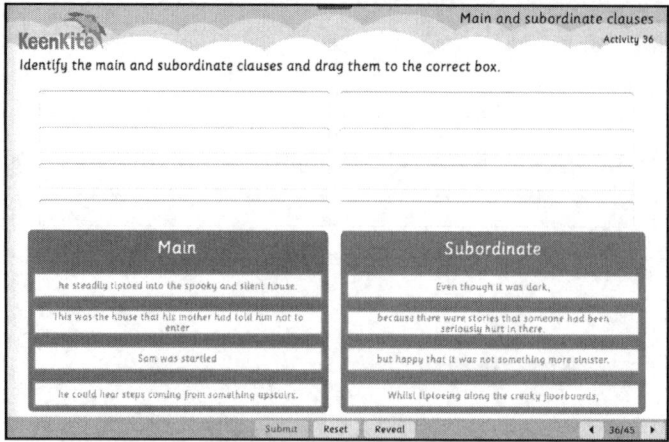

- Model identifying one example and discuss the subject (noun/proper noun/pronoun) and verb used in the examples.
- Highlight the main clause and the subordinate clause in the first example. Answers: *Even though it was dark* (subordinate clause) *he steadily tiptoed into the spooky and silent house* (main clause); *it was* – subject and verb; *he* and *tiptoed* – subject and verb.

Practise

- Ask pupils to think what might happen next, and then to write the second part of the narrative using main and subordinate clauses. Remind them to use descriptions to describe what they could see or how the character felt.

Apply

- Use a sentence starter to open the paragraph that comes after: *He took a deep breath and ventured up the stairs...*

Answers for pupil sheet

Activity 1:
   a. <u>When the road was clear</u>, Ali crossed to the other side.
   b. Rachel watched television <u>while her children tidied up the house</u>.
   c. Our horses go crazy <u>when cars drive past</u>.

Activity 2:

Sentence	Main clause	Subordinate clause
The policeman was annoyed <u>because the speeding car would not stop</u>.		✓
The house, <u>which has a red door</u>, has been empty for a year.		✓
<u>I always iron my shirts</u> before I wear them.	✓	

Activity 3:

Sentence	*after* used as a:	
	subordinating conjunction	preposition
The train ticket is cheaper after 9.30am in the morning.		✓
I had a long sleep after I had run the marathon.	✓	
Parking is free after 6 o'clock at night.		✓

Pupil sheet – Subordinate clauses and relative clauses

A subordinate clause provides extra information in a sentence. It would not make sense on its own because it is not a complete sentence. A subordinating conjunction is used to introduce a subordinate clause.

A relative clause is a special type of subordinate clause introduced by a relative pronoun. For example, *who, whom, which, that*. In general, we use *who, whom* and *whose* for people and *which* or *that* for non-human subjects.

Activity 1

Underline the subordinate clause in the sentences below.

Example:

Sarah enjoyed the pasta <u>because it was covered in tomato sauce</u>.

a. When the road was clear, Ali crossed to the other side.

b. Rachel watched television while her children tidied up the house.

c. Our horses go crazy when cars drive past.

Activity 2

Decide whether the underlined part of the sentence is a main clause or a subordinate clause. Tick **one** box in each row.

Sentence	Main clause	Subordinate clause
The policeman was annoyed <u>because the speeding car would not stop</u>.		
The house, <u>which has a red door</u>, has been empty for a year.		
<u>I always iron my shirts</u> before I wear them.		

Activity 3

Decide whether the word '**after**' is used as a subordinating conjunction or as a preposition in each sentence. Remember that a subordinate clause contains a subject (noun/proper noun/pronoun) and a verb. Tick **one** box in each row.

Sentence	*after* used as a:	
	subordinating conjunction	preposition
The train ticket is cheaper after 9.30am in the morning.		
I had a long sleep after I had run the marathon.		
Parking is free after 6 o'clock at night.		

Punctuation for parenthesis

By the end of Year 6, pupils are expected to be able to identify and use punctuation to indicate parenthesis. There are three ways that sentences can be punctuated to indicate parenthesis: brackets, dashes and commas. A parenthesis can be used to add an afterthought or comment, to add extra information or to give examples of a statement. The term 'parenthesis' is first introduced in Year 5 in the English programmes of study. Parenthesis can be single words, whole clauses or phrases.

Review

- Ask pupils what they understand by the term 'parenthesis'.
- Explain that writers can use brackets, dashes and commas to add extra information, to comment or to give examples.
- The sentence would make sense on its own without the extra information added to it.
- The extra information can also be a relative clause but this is not always the case.
- Using the interactive program, ask pupils to identify the correct use of brackets.

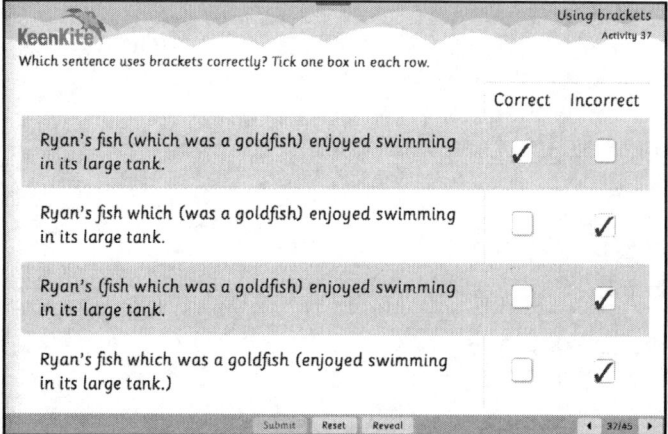

- Using the interactive program, ask pupils to insert commas in the sentence to indicate parenthesis.

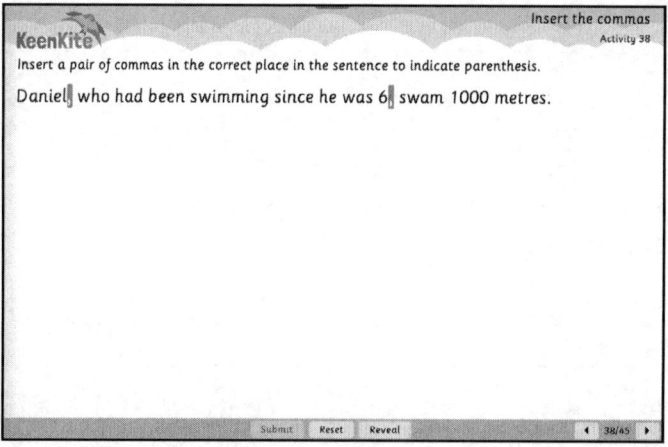

> **Sentence for modelling**
>
> Daniel, who had been swimming since he was 6, swam 1000 metres.

- Remind pupils that the sentence would make sense without the relative clause; for example: *Daniel swam 1000 metres*. The parenthesis part of the sentence – 'who had been swimming since he was 6' – is a relative clause (a type of subordinate clause) because it is introduced by the relative pronoun 'who'. It is a clause because it has the subject (noun or pronoun) 'who' and the verbs 'had been swimming' and 'was'.

Teach

- Introduce the example text – the thank you letter (see PDF13) – and highlight the section that says 'not to mention entertaining'. Explain that this not only adds more information but also adds a comment about how the writer felt.

Practise

- Using the interactive program, ask pupils to highlight examples of parenthesis that they can find within the text.

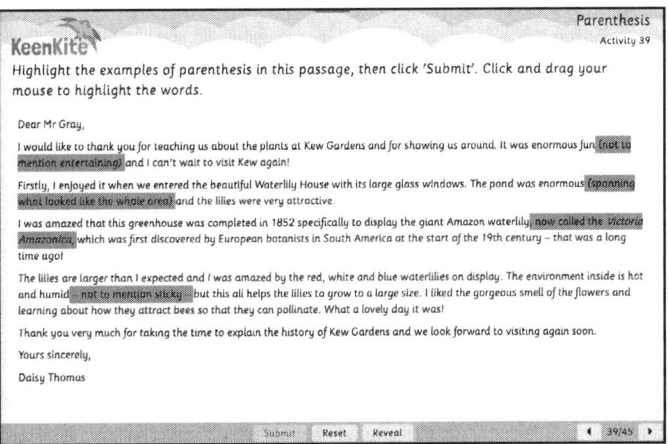

Apply

- Give pupils some sentences and ask them to add some extra information to make their sentences more exciting.

> **Example:**
>
> - Example sentences:
>   - *His trainers were the best in the shop.*
>   - *Kieran played the violin beautifully.*
>   - *Bradley couldn't wait to get home for dinner that evening.*
> - Example answers:
>   - *His trainers (which were white and gold) were the best in the shop.*
>   - *Kieran, who is 10 years old, played the violin beautifully.*
>   - *Bradley couldn't wait to get home for dinner (chicken and veg) that evening.*

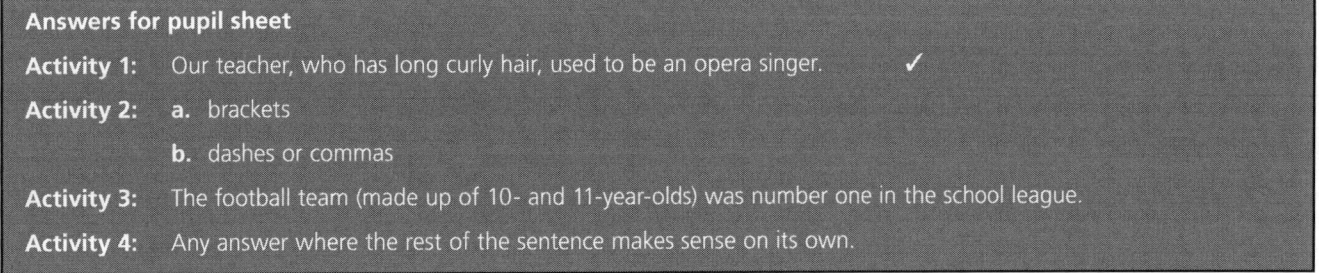

Answers for pupil sheet

Activity 1: Our teacher, who has long curly hair, used to be an opera singer. ✓

Activity 2: a. brackets

b. dashes or commas

Activity 3: The football team (made up of 10- and 11-year-olds) was number one in the school league.

Activity 4: Any answer where the rest of the sentence makes sense on its own.

Pupil sheet – Punctuation for parenthesis

Parenthesis can be used to add an afterthought or comment, to add extra information or to give examples of a statement. Parenthesis can be indicated by brackets, dashes or commas.

Activity 1

Which sentence uses commas correctly to add extra information?

Tick **one**

Our, teacher who has long curly hair, used to be an opera singer. ☐

Our teacher, who has long curly hair, used to be an opera singer. ☐

Our teacher who has, long curly hair, used to be an opera singer. ☐

Our teacher who has long curly hair, used to be an, opera singer. ☐

Activity 2

a. What is the name of the punctuation marks on either side of the words *'who was only 10 years old'* in the sentence below?

Ryan (who was only 10 years old) could run the 100 metre sprint in 12 seconds.

b. Name **two** punctuation marks that could be used to show parenthesis?

Activity 3

Insert a pair of brackets ( ) into the sentence in the correct place to show parenthesis.

The football team made up of 10- and 11-year-olds was number one in the school league.

Activity 4

Write your own sentence using a parenthesis. Remember that the sentence must make sense without the parenthesis.

Active and passive voice

By the end of Year 6, pupils should be able to identify and use the active and passive voice. In the passive voice, the subject of the sentence in the active voice becomes the object. The passive voice is mainly used in formal writing.

Review

- Ask pupils what they understand by the terms 'active' and 'passive'.
- Explain that in the active voice, the subject is doing the action but in the passive voice, the subject becomes the object of the sentence.
- *David* (subject) *ate* (verb) *a biscuit* (object). → *The biscuit* (subject) *was eaten* (verb) *by David*.
- The object of the sentence can be introduced by the word '*by*'. However, sometimes the object is not indicated; for example, *The biscuits were eaten*.
- The passive voice contains the verb 'to be'; for example, *is*, *are*, *was*, *were* and the past participle of the verb (for example, *spoken*, *cleaned*, *finished*): *The cupboards were cleaned by Mum*.
- Using the interactive program, ask pupils to identify the active and passive sentences.

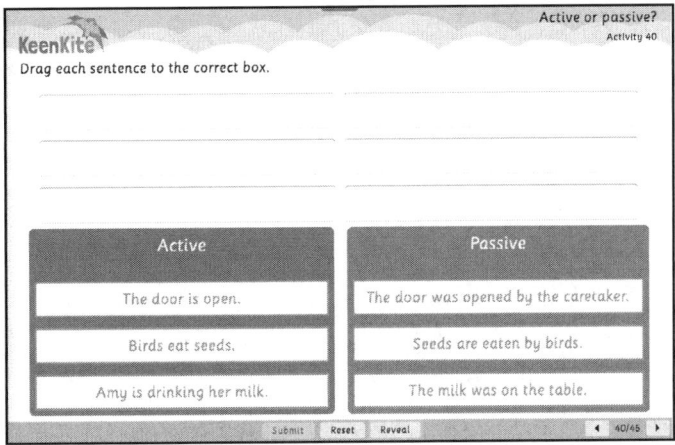

> **Sentence for modelling**
>
> *Birds* (subject) *eat* (verb) *seeds* (object). → *Seeds* (subject) *are eaten* (verb phrase) *by birds* (object).

- Underline the subject and object of the sentence and show how the subject becomes the object of the sentence in the passive.
- Model some more examples to pupils.
- Using the interactive program, ask pupils to match the correct sentence beginnings with the endings to make passive voice statements.

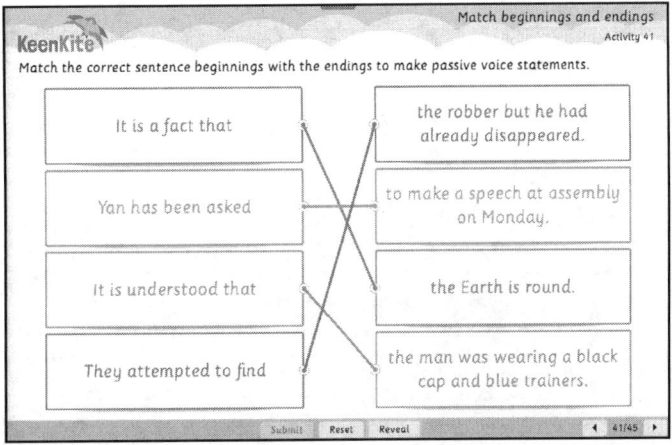

- Explain to pupils that sometimes the passive is written in another way. It can be written with the word 'to': *attempt to, propose to, endeavour to, begin to.*
- Some passive verb forms can also start with 'it'; for example, *It is thought that these animals were considered to have been extinct nearly 1000 years ago.*

Teach

- Introduce pupils to the example text of the news report *Plane Crash* (see PDF14).
- Model selecting the correct active voice.

Practise

- Using the interactive program, ask pupils to match the passive phrase to its active equivalent.

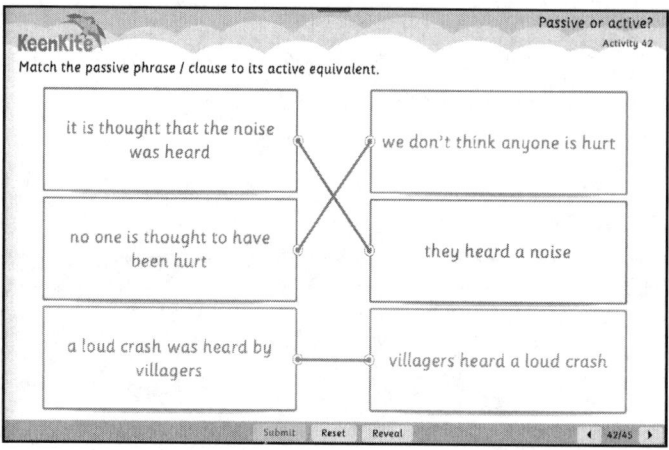

Apply

- Play the 'Speaking and Listening' game. Ask pupils to work in pairs.
- One pupil says a sentence in the active voice and the partner replies in the passive voice.
- Then ask pupils to swap over. For example:
  Partner 1: *Ryan ate an orange.*
  Partner 2: *The orange was eaten by Ryan.*

Answers for pupil sheet

Activity 1:

Sentence	Active	Passive
Grass is eaten by cows.		✓
Owls hunt at night.	✓	
Zebras are hunted by lions.		✓
Monkeys are playful creatures.	✓	
The orange was eaten by Tom.		✓

Activity 2:

Active	Passive
The head teacher opened the door.	The door was opened by the head teacher.
Fay ate the apple.	The apple was eaten by Fay.
Tom read the book.	The book was read by Tom.
Isabel washed the dishes.	The dishes were washed by Isabel.

Activity 3: The engaging and funny show was enjoyed by the children.

Activity 4: The head teacher announced the winners.

Pupil sheet – Active and passive voice

In the active voice, the subject is doing the action, but in the passive voice, the subject becomes the object of the sentence.

David (subject) *ate* (verb) *a biscuit* (object).   ➜   *The biscuit* (subject) *was eaten* (verb) *by David*.

In the passive voice, the object is not always required. For example: *The biscuits were eaten.*

Activity 1

Which sentences are written in the passive voice and which in the active? Tick the correct boxes. The first one has been done for you.

Sentence	Active	Passive
Grass is eaten by cows.		✓
Owls hunt at night.		
Zebras are hunted by lions.		
Monkeys are playful creatures.		
The orange was eaten by Tom.		

Activity 2

Change these sentences from active to passive. The first one has been done for you.

Active	Passive
The head teacher opened the door.	The door was opened by the head teacher.
Fay ate the apple.	
Tom read the book.	
Isabel washed the dishes.	

Activity 3

Rewrite the sentence below in the passive voice.

The children enjoyed the engaging and funny show.

The engaging and funny

Activity 4

Rewrite the sentence below so that it is in the active voice. Remember to punctuate the sentence correctly.

The winners were announced by the head teacher.

Subjunctive verb form

By the end of Year 6, pupils are expected to know the difference between structures typical of informal speech and structures appropriate for formal speech and writing. They need to understand that the subjunctive form can be used in formal writing and speeches. For example: *If I were to change schools, I would be upset. Were they to visit, we would organise a party.*

Review

- Explain to pupils that the subjunctive mood can be used to express an imaginary situation, a wish, a demand or a hypothesis.
- 'As though' can be used to compare something that is not actually happening. For example: *He ran across the street as though a pack of wolves were chasing him.*
- Pupils can use 'if' and 'wish' with the verb 'were' to express a wish or hypothetical situation. For example: *If I were on the school council, I would ensure that we had longer playtimes. I wish I were free to attend your party but it is my father's birthday that day.*
- Using the interactive program, ask pupils to choose a verb to complete the sentences so that they use the subjunctive form.

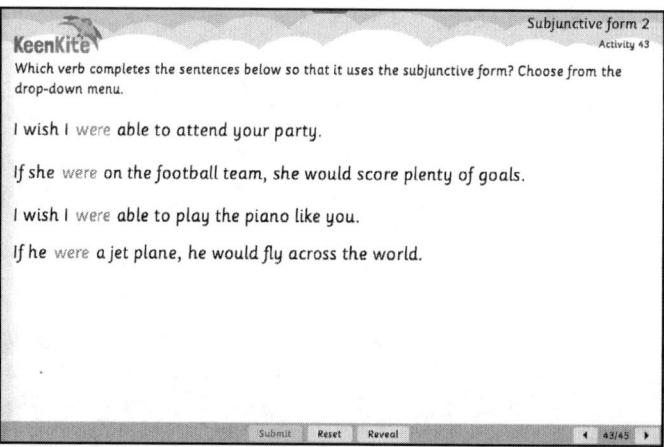

- Explain that the subjunctive mode can also use the word 'that' after a formal verb; for example, *suggest that, required that, proposes that.*
- Using the interactive program, ask pupils to match the beginnings and ends of the sentences so that the sentence contains the subjunctive form.

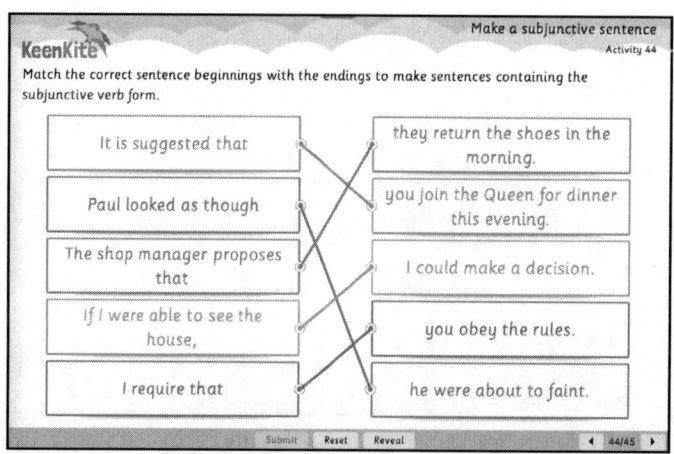

Teach

- Show pupils the example poem *I wish I were...* (see PDF15).
- Highlight the sentence, '*I wish I were a butterfly*'.
- Explain to pupils that in the subjunctive form, writers and speakers can use the word 'were' instead of 'was'.

Practise

- Using the interactive program, ask pupils to insert the correct verb into the sentence so that it uses the subjunctive form.

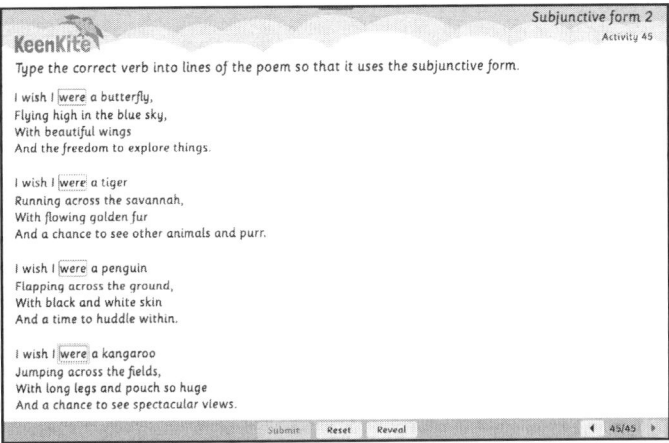

Apply

- Give pupils a selection of animals and ask them to write one verse of a poem using a similar style to the example text: lion, panda, squirrel, cat, fish, zebra, peacock.
- Some pupils may require pictures of the animals to stimulate their thoughts and ideas.

Answers for pupil sheet

Activity 1:
a. I wish I were able to join everyone, but I have another appointment.
b. Were I to be elected as a member of the school council, I would ensure we had a new playground built.
c. She ran across the playground as though a pack of wolves were chasing her.

Activity 2:

	(Tick one)
could be	
were	✓
was	
may be	

Activity 3:

Sentence	Subjunctive form	
	Used	Not used
I wish I were famous.	✓	
My suitcase is heavy because I have plenty of shoes.		✓
Lisa has many hobbies.		✓

Activity 4: Accept any sentence that makes sense.

Pupil sheet – Subjunctive verb form

The subjunctive mood can be used to express an imaginary situation, a wish, a demand or a hypothesis. It is used in formal speech and writing. Writers can use 'if' and 'wish' with the verb 'were' to express a wish or hypothetical situation.

The subjunctive mood can also use the word 'that' after a formal verb. For example: *it is suggested that, it is required that, it is proposed that*. The subjunctive is used to make a suggestion.

Activity 1

Which option completes the sentences below so that they use the subjunctive mood?

| were | it is suggested that | I were | were I |

> **Example:**
>
> <u>It is suggested that</u> you join the Queen for lunch next week.

a. I wish _____ able to join everyone, but I have another appointment.

b. _____ to be elected as a member of the school council, I would ensure we had a new playground built.

c. She ran across the playground as though a pack of wolves _____ chasing her.

Activity 2

Which option completes the sentence so that it uses the subjunctive form?

I wish I _____ able to attend, but I have classes that day.

	(Tick **one**)
could be	
were	
was	
may be	

Activity 3

Decide whether the sentence uses the subjunctive form or not. Tick **one** box in each row.

Sentence	Subjunctive form	
	Used	Not used
I wish I were famous.		
My suitcase is heavy because I have plenty of shoes.		
Lisa has many hobbies.		

Activity 4

Complete the sentence below with an ending that makes sense.

I wish I were _____